Plus One
Plus None

Confessions of a 40-something single
& what not to do so you don't
end up single in your 40s

Emica Mao

Copyright © 2019 Emica Mao

All rights reserved.

ISBN: 9781081809560

DEDICATION

To all single women,

May this book remind you to –

reinforce your goals and wishes with action,
embrace your situation and imperfections with thoughtful reflection,
and go for whatever it is that you want in life even if sometimes, it's a path less taken.

PREFACE

Plus One Plus None is based on the true story of a woman named Zita. She's candid, analytical, funny and unapologetically single.

Her upbringing, values, beliefs, personality, cultural idiosyncrasies and circumstances may be different from yours, but the thought process of asking yourself a lot of whys in life, doing what needs to be done to achieve something, and accepting the consequences of your decisions and actions - are all universal. You can use all of these principles not just in your single situation, but at whatever life stage you are in, and in the pursuit of your dreams and goals.

May Zita's story nudge you to examine your own situation, to think about what you really want to happen in your life, and more importantly, to start making things happen in your life.

Emica Mao

1 LINEAR PATH

Hi, I'm Zita. I am a forty-something single. Wait, hold your thought for a second. If you are still single and you are above 30 but younger than 40, I bet this was your instant thought bubble when I said I am forty-something –

Phew, Zita is still single and she's older than me!
Why you …
Just kidding. It's okay. I'm good even if you are deriving joy and relief at the expense of my mature age. For whatever reason, when you meet someone who is single and older than you are, you feel a little less pressured. I guess it's because your mind automatically concludes that relative to the other person who is older, she is certainly more pressured to get hitched sooner than you are.

So, let me guess what were your other secret thought bubbles…
She is 40-plus?! She could be my mom already!
Whew, I still have xx more years before I turn 40…
I would definitely get hitched before I reach 40.
Forty-plus? I should be married with 3 kids by then.

Bring it on. Just remember, one day, you will also be in your forties. But don't worry, you can still continue to derive joy and relief from me because I would be a grandma by then. ;-)

I am sure your big question for me is – why am I still single? Did I plan to be single at 40? When I was in my twenties, is this what I have envisioned? Or did a guy break my heart that I gave up on love? Or am I just unlucky in love? No, no and no.

When I was in my 20s, my vision of my 40-year old self was that I would be married with kids. So what happened, right? Why didn't that materialize? Let me tell you my story and hopefully after reading my story, you would figure out what you need to do in your life today especially if you don't want to end up unmarried in your 40s like me. ;-)

*****

When I was growing up, I thought life followed a linear path. You go to school and get a degree, work in your twenties, and once you are financially stable in your mid-twenties to early thirties, you get married and have kids. And then you will live happily ever after... or at least figure out the rest of your life with your husband. This is the same life path my parents had, and it is the common storyline of most romantic movies I have watched as a young adult.

My life followed a linear path until the financially stable part. I became financially stable in my mid-twenties all right, but after that, the storyline I knew as a kid did not happen. Unexpected circumstances derailed me from the linear path as I realized there are a lot of things in life that don't come easily or that don't just happen naturally, like meeting your special someone.

In movies, people serendipitously meet prospects in all kinds of places - parks, hospitals, coffee shops, supermarkets, bookstores, gyms, airports, name it. And random strangers strike conversations with each other like it's the most natural thing to do.

A girl accidentally drops a book and a guy picks it up for her and that starts a conversation.

A girl attends a party and meets a friend of the host and they just hit it off.

Two strangers sit together on a plane, they make small talk and by the end of the flight, they are inseparable.

Well, guess what? I have accidentally dropped so many things - not just books but pens, coins, ice cream, a can of baked beans, and even a big watermelon. I have spent thousands of hours browsing through books in bookstores, walking in parks, and waiting in line at supermarket counters. And I have been on many flights, train rides, bus rides and car-sharing rides. Nothing close to any of the boy-meets-girl movie scenes has ever happened.

Okay, maybe there are a few serendipitous meetings in my life, but nothing has progressed to a full-blown episode. And my serendipitous scenes are more satirical than romantic.

Case in point – I was in Singapore one weekend and I spent the afternoon at the National Museum. I had a heavy lunch and could feel that sleepiness was slowly creeping on me. As I was looking at a painting and just as when I was about to yawn, a guy approached me and asked -

Hi! Do you like history?

Such impeccable timing! Sadly, when I faced him, it was too late for me to stifle my yawn. After yawning right in front of his face, how can I even tell him that yes, I like history?!

This is just one of the many comical moments in my life. More to come later.

But going back to another thing which I did not expect wouldn't come as easily and naturally (at least based on my naive mind and myopic vision from my childhood) was meeting eligible prospects.

In movies, eligible guys appear in a girl's life simultaneously or they appear one after another. Almost always, they also come into someone's life at the right time. Most too are good-looking, charming, well-mannered, kind, generous, smart, funny and yes, almost perfect. In short, there's both quantity and quality of prospects.

In real life, prospects come in trickles. They appear in your life intermittently and sporadically. And almost always, they are not your types. There's scarcity and a lot of unpredictability.

Such a huge gap between reality versus expectation! I only realized all of these as an adult - specifically in my early thirties - when year in and year out, the flow of quantity and quality prospects which I was expecting never happened.

But before dissecting that part of my life, let's first backtrack to an earlier time - the period when I haven't realized yet there was a huge disparity between reality versus expectation, primarily because I was still right on track on the linear path.

When I was 25 (yes, around the same time I became financially stable), I also got into my first serious relationship which you could say was somehow accidental. First boyfriend at 25?! Please don't judge me but I'll explain shortly why I had my first relationship only in my mid-twenties.

Anyway, I had this *boy <space> friend* - a term I like to call my guy platonic friends. I did not know this particular *boy <space> friend* liked me in a special way. I am not the type of person who assumes anything unless the other person explicitly tells me something. Yes, I'm a bit dense with the romance department.

The first time I discovered this *boy <space> friend* liked me in a special way was when he invited me to go out. A few blocks away from my place, he stopped the car to get something from the trunk but before he got out of the car, he told me he accidentally dropped something under my seat earlier and asked me if I can reach underneath to get it. When I did, I felt something long, thin and with rough protrusions and leaves. *Uh-oh...* I froze.

When he got back to the driver's seat and asked me if I found what he dropped, I told him –

Oh, there's nothing under my seat.

I had to lie because I did not know how to react!

He asked me to reach underneath again and I had no choice but to pull out the thing. It was a long-stemmed red rose stripped of its thorns. I didn't see this coming, so I did not know what to say. I babbled –

Oh no, what's this?

It was super awkward.

Anyway, I gave him the benefit of the doubt because he could just be playing a prank on me, right? But at each of our stopovers, he gave me a red rose. When we reached our final destination, he gave me all the rest. I ended up getting twenty-four red roses that day.

This *boy* <space> *friend* patiently courted me. He knew for instance I did not want my colleagues to know he was pursuing me because I did not want to be teased in the office. Guess what he did one time when he picked me up from work? He wore a wig! When I asked him why he was wearing a wig, he said that he was in disguise, so my colleagues won't recognize him. Well, it was so effective that even I wasn't able to recognize him!

Then among his many sweet gestures, once, he sent me huge flower arrangements every day for a week - red Ecuadorian roses, tulips, carnations, chrysanthemums, birds of paradise, daisies and even blue roses. But in as much as I appreciate flowers, I told him to stop sending me flowers because I know they cost a lot for something that only lasts for a few days. Besides, I get the same joy from looking at pictures of flowers.

The following week he sent me an unusual-looking bouquet. It was all green leaves, no flowers. It was a big bunch of spinach beautifully wrapped with pink tissue paper!

That same evening, he called me and asked –

So, did you like the bouquet I sent today?

I replied -

It's what I am having now for dinner.

Yes, seriously. I love spinach and I sautéed it with garlic.

There was also one time when *boy <space> friend* sent someone to my office to deliver a telegram. I found it odd because I know telegrams are already obsolete. (To most of you though, I am sure the only telegram you know is the chat app.)

Anyway, I told the delivery guy I will just get a pen to sign the receiving copy, but the guy said that what he needed was an electric socket, not a pen, which I found even weirder. I pointed to the nearest socket and the next thing I knew the guy was setting up a mini karaoke and he started playing music and singing. It was a singing telegram! The same singer came to serenade me every day for one whole week. It became a mid-afternoon spectacle in the office. It was super embarrassing.

But wait, before you get carried away with all the romantic gestures, let me cut the story short and tell you why I said the relationship was accidental. Accidental because one night, when we went out, *boy <space> friend* did not want to bring me home until I said yes to formalizing our relationship. When I wasn't budging, he offered me a 3-month trial period. I'm not kidding! He said we can try it out for 3 months and if I wanted out after that period, he would accept my decision. I'm not kidding too when I tell you I said yes to the trial period because I was so tired and sleepy, and I badly wanted to go home to sleep already.

The next morning, I told him the truth - that I did not

mean what I said the previous night and that I only said yes because I wanted to go home and sleep. He insisted that the trial period was on and that I cannot back out until it's over. It became official. I had to drop the "space" - *boy <space> friend* became *boyfriend*.

I had difficulty shifting from a platonic to a romantic relationship. It felt super weird and awkward just to hold hands. The first time he said, "*I love you*", I replied, "*Thank you*". The first time he said, "*I miss you*", I replied "*Okay*". It took some time before I could reply back "*I love you*" and "*I miss you too*". Until then, it was one embarrassing thing to another.

But because of the trial period, I realized that feelings could be developed over time. When the shift happened (which was still within the 3-month trial period), there was no more awkwardness and weirdness. Everything was just like in the movies - everything he did was cuteness overload, everything he said was super funny and amusing, and every little gesture he made was heart-melting. And yes, I was able to say, "*I love you*" and "*I miss you*" all the time. I can be normal after all.

To overwrite the 3-month trial proposal in the car, he made a more romantic proposal after I'd adjusted and this time it was atop a lighthouse. *Awww...* (Actually, it wasn't really an *awww* moment for me because I fear heights which he didn't know until we reached the top of the tower.)

I know the 3-month trial story sounds ridiculous but guess what? Three months got stretched to three years! Not bad for something I got into because I was tired and sleepy one night.

*****

Having a boyfriend when you are young is really good but only if you truly know yourself.

In my case, when I got into a serious relationship, I

pretty much did not have a good sense of my identity. I didn't know yet what I wanted in life, so I became a chameleon. I began to like what he liked. His favorites became my favorites. It was so terrible up to the point where I stopped eating my favorite fried chicken just because he liked another fried chicken place. Yes, seriously.

One day, I chanced upon Julia Roberts' movie, *Runaway Bride*, and it hit me - I don't know how I like my eggs cooked!

Is it hard-boiled?
Soft boiled?
Hard scrambled?
Soft scrambled?
Sunny side up?
Poached?
I had no idea.

I also realized that when I got into our relationship, I stopped seeing my other friends. Only a couple of them actually met *boyfriend* so to many of them, they may have thought that *boyfriend* was just a figment of my imagination.

I also stopped trying out new things. All the activities I did were with him.

I stopped growing outside of the relationship.

I felt I needed time to discover myself and explore new things on my own.

But I had a lot of fears too. To break up or not to break up with him? That was the big question.

When I was thinking about breaking up with *boyfriend*, I was about to turn 29. I was in my late twenties – an age when a lot of your friends are already married, or are engaged, or are in stable relationships that are marriage bound. Twenty-nine was well within a girl's prime years - a perfect age to marry, get pregnant and have children based on the linear storyline.

You could just imagine what kind of fears and unpleasant thoughts occupied my head for weeks as I contemplated the future.

What if I never find someone else?

What if there will be no other guy who would be as thoughtful and creative as to come up with sending me a spinach bouquet? Yes, I must hand it to *boyfriend* for being both romantically creative and creatively romantic.

What if I am making a big mistake and regret it later on?

What if I become lonely and depressed?

What if I won't be able to marry on time?

What if I marry late and have difficulty getting pregnant?

What if I marry really late and never have kids?

What if I never marry and become a spinster?

I told my closest friends about my dilemma. There was *Team Work It Out* and *Team Get Out Of It*.

One thing I learned about making decisions is sometimes deep within us, we have a secret answer already even before we seek advice (though we would probably never admit this). Then when we ask our friends for advice, we selectively pick pieces of advice that affirm our secret decision even if there are glaring and more compelling reasons we should do otherwise.

I've seen friends who have made this mistake and I swear, there is no amount of logic, not even common sense, that would convince them to see the light. Here's a sample conversation where I've seen this no-amount-of-logic-can-penetrate-a-person no matter how compelling an argument is:

Me: *But he cheated on you 5 times already!*
Friend: *He promised this will be the last time.*
Me: *But that's what he told you too the last 4 times!*
Friend: *This time it will be different.*
Me: *But he's still seeing girl #3 & #4!*
Friend: *He said those are just platonic relationships.*

Unbelievable, right? Conversations like this make you want to pound your friend's head really hard to bring her back to her senses.

To make sure I won't be as logically blind and deaf, and I have the mental clarity to make the right decision, I had to start with a blank slate. I had to set aside my fears, otherwise, I might choose the option which would address my fears. I also had to remind myself that I wasn't a drama queen so why was I having these out-of-character thoughts suddenly? It was not the end of the world. And why was I even worrying about not having kids when I wasn't really sure if I wanted to get married in the first place?

I remember during an earlier stage of our relationship, *boyfriend* hypothetically asked me if I would say yes to a secret marriage with him. I said no. It was still a no even if the hypothetical situation weren't a secret marriage. That was when we were still at our giddiest and any person crazy in love would probably say yes to anything, but I consistently said no even if it were just hypothetical. Anyway, he had not brought up any marriage question since then so why was I even worrying about marriage? Maybe he didn't even have marriage plans anymore.

The scenarios playing in my head were way ahead of their time when the only issue I had to deal with was - should I or should I not break up with him?

To simplify things, I only had to ask myself - what is my end goal in having a relationship? For me, it's marriage. Then as a follow-up question, I asked myself what does marriage mean to me? I'm very traditional so it's *'til death do us part* for me. If I don't end up with the right person, marriage could be a lifetime trap. *Shudder.*

A lifetime trap is a terrifying thought! This means I have to be really sure not just about him but about myself too, and clearly, I wasn't sure about myself.

This simple realization made it easy for me to decide. All my other fears seemed immaterial versus the fear of ending up with the wrong person because I don't know myself enough.

Also, at that point in our relationship, the fuzzy feeling had dissipated. Calls, messages, and dates became less frequent. Sweet gestures came by in small trickles. Some traits I found adorable in him before weren't as adorable anymore. We were just three years in the relationship, and it was already like that. It can only get worse once we're married. My instinct told me that at that point, he was also just probably waiting for me to initiate the breakup. So, one evening, I initiated the talk and we said our goodbyes. *Boyfriend* became *boy <tab, tab, tab> friend*.

I was probably right about him waiting for me to initiate the breakup because after the breakup, he never attempted to get back together. He did occasionally keep in touch in the first couple of years, but I think it was more out of curiosity.

The best years of my life (and probably his life too) started since then.

Can you guess what I did on the first week right after our breakup? I ate at my favorite fried chicken place every day for one whole week!

In retrospect, if I ended up getting married in my twenties, I would have been separated in my thirties because the more I got to know myself after the breakup, the more I realized that *boy <tab, tab, tab> friend* and I weren't a good match.

Plus One Plus None

2 REBOOT

I remember hearing a story about someone who, one day, overheard his dad and his dad's friends talking about their regrets in life. They rattled off a lot of things, which in retrospect, they think they should have done when they were much younger. Sadly, they could no longer pursue those activities because they were already old and physically weak.

This story resurfaced into my consciousness when I was ready to reboot my life. As a first step towards refocusing on myself after the breakup, I wrote down what I wanted in life as a preventive measure against having regrets later on. My list included:

- Places I want to visit
- Skills I want to learn
- Goals I want to accomplish
- Material things I want to own
- Wishes I want to come true

I called it my *Do-While-I-Can List* or *DWIC* List for short. I didn't want to name it the usual *Things Before I Die* List or *bucket list* because this connotes that you have a full lifetime to pursue the things on your list, so the tendency is for you to either –

(1) keep putting them off knowing you still have lots of years ahead of you to do them; or

(2) you will only actively pursue them when you are about to kick the bucket.

The reality is we have different life spans, energy levels, and physical conditions. Some of us may complete a lifetime without reaching old age, and some of us may no longer be physically able to do certain activities even before reaching our prime years. Thus, the DWIC List. Just do whatever you can while you can still do them.

My DWIC List was about 70% wants and 30% wishes. Wants are generally goals where there is a clear path of making them happen if I do my part such as taking up lessons, consistently practicing, and setting aside funds to afford them.

Wishes, on the other hand, are things which I have no idea how to make happen. I don't know if 10,000 hours of brainstorming, planning, praying and practice would bring me any closer to making them come true but there is no harm in adding them to my DWIC List. Maybe I'll figure out how to make them happen eventually or I'll just get lucky.

Let me give you a sneak peek of my initial DWIC List and how I fared...

*****

Learn photography. I like looking at beautiful photos so I thought I should learn photography.

One day, I saw an announcement about a photography tour to a beautiful island - a perfect opportunity to learn photography and do some sightseeing. I emailed the organizer to check if I can join even if I have never attended any formal photography class. The organizer said yes and so I signed up for the photo trip.

The day arrived and I went to the meeting place. As soon as I saw the other participants, I got nervous. Everyone was bringing big bulky camera bags and I had no camera bag because ... my camera was just inside the pocket of my jeans! Luckily, there was a couple who brought along their three kids age 5, 9 and 12 who also had point and shoot cameras. *Phew*, I wasn't alone. But I had to stay very close to the kids throughout the photo trip.

One thing I discovered though about myself after joining several photography tours and trying out various camera equipment (yes, I bought a DSLR camera eventually) was - I simply want to take photos, not necessarily take the perfect shot.

Trying to take the perfect shot may sometimes prevent you from seeing the finer details of the subject as you are more concerned with composition, contrast, and exposure, among many other things. How did I realize this? Once on a trip, I got asked by a friend if I noticed how the tiny dark violet stripes against the yellow petal of the flowers (we saw earlier in the day) looked so beautiful. I thought for a moment – what is she talking about? Were there tiny stripes on the petals? I only remember seeing white, violet and yellow petals, but no other details. I had to review my photos to see the tiny stripes my friend was talking about. What a pity I only saw what she was talking about in a photo and not the real thing while I was right in front of it.

Taking the perfect shot may also consume a lot of time that you miss out on the real moment of appreciating the subject as it happens, such as watching a beautiful sunset or watching a bunch of kids play. When we're so wrapped up with our attempts to take the perfect shot, there is a tendency that at the end of the day, our memories are merely compilations of subjects as seen through the camera lens, not with our own eyes. I want my memories to be of moments I have witnessed with my own eyes and the purpose of my not-so-perfect photos are just to serve as reminders of these memories.

*****

Speak a foreign language. I love Japan and Japanese stuff - *furoshiki*, origami, cherry blossoms, washi tape, toilet seats with multiple bidet functions, beautiful manhole covers, the *kanban* method, shabu-shabu, ramen - among many other Japanese things. Because of this fascination for Japanese, I took up Nihongo language classes.

Several months later, we had a bunch of Japanese guests and I was so excited to put into practice my Nihongo learnings. I told them I know a little Nihongo and they were all excited to hear some phrases. Suddenly, my mind went blank! I just said whatever came to my mind which was -

Watashiwa ... ahh... hmmm... buta des ka.

All of them burst into laughter! I was puzzled and I asked them what was so funny, but no one could answer me because they were laughing so hard. They were all in tears! Finally, when one of the Japanese recovered from laughter, he told me –

You just said that you are a pig.

Of all the Japanese words that I could remember, why was "*buta*" at the top of my head???

*****

Learn a sport and get into fitness activities.

I've never been athletic. I played softball and table tennis in middle school but only because my class lacked players to complete a team in these two sports.

What sports and fitness activities did I try during the reboot? I learned how to play golf and guess what? I bagged trophies for being the second runner-up not just in one, but in three golf tournaments! Wow, right?!

How I wish I could just end my golf story with that since my track record sounds so impressive. Sadly, the only reason I won those trophies was that there were only three female players in all the three tournaments which made me – *ta-dah* - the second runner-up by default in the ladies' division!

What else did I try? Tennis, badminton, Pilates, Bikram Yoga, ballroom dancing, hip-hop dancing, jazz dancing…

Jazz dancing! That just brought back some memories.

So, I enrolled in a jazz dancing class and during the first session, I discovered that most of my classmates were professional dancers in a television show. *Gulp.*

At the end of the session, our dance instructor asked us to individually do the chasse across the room. The room was like 15 meters long. *Shudder.*

Have I mentioned to you that I'm not graceful at all? My body is super stiff.

What happened? In as much as it was nerve-racking for me to do the chasse, I think it was more painful for my classmates to watch my cringe-inducing performance as I glided across the full stretch of 15 meters like a robot. It was one of those moments you wished the ground would open up and just swallow you.

After class, as I was packing my stuff, a brave soul approached me and said –

Hey, don't worry about today. When I started, I was worse than you.

Lol. I know he meant well but guess what? That just validated how terribly bad I was!

*****

Travel. When you're single, married friends usually advise you to maximize traveling opportunities while you're still single because traveling becomes more challenging when you have kids as you must wait until your kids reach a certain age before you can comfortably travel again.

You will hear similar advice from elderly retirees but for a different reason. Their version is for you to travel while you are young and energetic because when you are already old, long-haul flights, commuting, navigating, walking, hiking, among many other things, could be really challenging as you may already have arthritis, cataract, incontinence, etc. You may have all the money when you are old, they say, but what will you do with your money if you can no longer do the things you want to do?

Given these nuggets of wisdom, several items on my DWIC List were travel destinations. As of my last count, I have visited 35 countries. Some of my most memorable adventures include:

- exploring Angkor Wat and other ancient temples in Siem Reap, Cambodia;
- getting awestruck by the Lost City of Petra, Jordan;
- finding my way (or rather getting lost) in a giant maze in Tasmania, Australia. At closing time, when it was already getting dark, a staff member had to fetch me right in the middle of the maze because I couldn't find my way out;
- going inside a pyramid in Egypt;
- swimming in the Dead Sea;
- glacier hiking in Iceland;
- diving with whale sharks in the Philippines;
- being mesmerized by the Cathedral of Santiago de Compostela in Spain,
- visiting an underground salt mine in Poland;
- going on a pilgrimage tour in Israel;
- exploring the archaeological excavations of Pompeii in Italy;
- attending the Papal Easter Mass at St. Peter's Basilica in Vatican City;
- enjoying the beautiful beaches and the chill vibe of Waikiki, Hawaii;
- getting wonderstruck by the Westminster Abbey and enjoying musicals at London's West End; and

- seeing Japan's beautiful cherry blossoms and Mount Fuji and eating all my favorite Japanese food. Yum!

There are just so many beautiful places to see around the world. Thanks to airline seat sales, free walking tours, and budget accommodations, traveling is now affordable more than ever for commoners like me.

*****

Take art lessons. I like looking at paintings and artworks, but I have no artistic talent. But then I realized that I never had formal training either. Maybe if I get lessons, some hidden talent would be uncovered. Besides, it's never too late to learn, right? Winston Churchill, for instance, started painting when he was in his forties. Throughout his lifetime, he finished over 500 artworks.

Inspired by this, I got into acrylic painting. After learning the basic painting techniques, our teacher asked us to paint our first artwork and so I searched online for some inspiration. Since it would be my first artwork, I wanted to do something that was not too difficult because if I cannot achieve what I want on my first attempt, I might easily give up.

After I completed my first painting, I showed it to my colleagues. Their eyes instantly lit up! Promising sign. I have potential, I thought.

But their delight was followed by similar comments –
Wow, it's Cookie Monster!
Is that Cookie Monster??
Your version of Cookie Monster looks really cute!
Awww... I love Cookie Monster!

The thing was - my subject was not Cookie Monster! Cookie Monster was not even on my mind when I was painting the artwork.

After all those comments, I named my first masterpiece as "*Monsterpiece*".

*****

I wasn't able to do things like these when I was in a relationship because I reserved most of my free time to make sure I was always available when *boyfriend* asked me out. It was my definition of being able to devote *"quality time"*.

In hindsight, there's a simpler way to devote *"quality time"* without depriving yourself of living your own life – just agree on a schedule or pre-plan.

Anyway, looking back at my earliest version of my DWIC List, I may not have succeeded in most of my attempts and my hidden talents (if any at all) still remain hidden, but what's important is that I tried and that I relentlessly continue to try and learn new things.

3 TICK TOCK

During the reboot, I had the time of my life. I did whatever I wanted to do whenever and with whomever. Total freedom. Pure bliss.

I forgot about the time. I forgot about the linear storyline. My storyline became more like a choose-your-own-adventure type.

Tick tock ... tick tock ...

Until one day, I noticed that my calendar was packed with weddings, baptisms and children's parties.

Tick tock ... tick tock ...

Until one day, I realized most of my friends were married or are getting married.

Tick tock ... tick tock ...

Until one day, I could get none of my usual travel buddies to join me on trips because they could not leave their babies with their husbands.

Tick tock ... tick tock ...

Until one day, I overheard someone tag me as a spinster for the first time! *Shudder.*

One of my cousins was getting married and the upcoming occasion triggered a conversation among my aunts. I overheard them doing a quick check on who else was still unmarried from my generation and *BOOM*! I heard my name. I was officially classified as an old maid.

Tick tock ... tick tock ...

Until one day I bumped into the kids from my childhood - babies I saw in their diapers and carried in my arms, toddlers I saw learning how to walk and talk, and smaller kids I played with when I was a kid myself. I used to tower over them all and by the sheer difference in our heights, I thought our age gap was huge! I felt I was way more advanced in life than them.

Fast forward to when I saw them - some were already taller than me and some even had their own kids in tow! The innocent kids of my childhood are now way more advanced in life than me. Here I am - I am not married, I have not given birth, I have not raised kids and I have not managed a household beyond one person.

I wonder –

Where have all the years gone by???

I was 33.

Wakey-wakey! It was time for me to get back on my feet and get back on track since I took a very long detour. I enjoyed the reboot so much I forgot all about the linear storyline.

Besides all the wake-up calls, there also came a barrage of pokes and nudges wherever I went –

Where is your Plus One?
When will you have a Plus One?
How come you have no Plus One?
Are you seeing anyone?
Why are you still single?
Why don't you have a boyfriend?
What do you do on weekends?
Don't you ever get lonely?
Are you too picky? If you stay picky, you'll be alone forever.
Your friend xx just got married. Are you next?
All your friends are getting hitched. How about you?
The longer you wait, the harder it is to get pregnant.

Have you considered freezing your eggs?
You are not getting any younger. What are you still waiting for?
Blah-blah.

I was 33 but honestly, I thought and felt still young. But what if they were right that I was not getting any younger? I had to do something. I must put myself out there, but I did not know where to start. I had to take a refresher course on dating. Ooops, wrong word. It's inaccurate to use the word "*refresher*" because there is nothing to refresh from my memory in the first place.

It is very embarrassing to admit but I've always sucked at dating. I know of people who could easily warm up to others and get asked out for dates after the first conversation. I'm definitely not one of them.

Because I am an introvert, I don't like to share information about myself and I evade personal questions, ergo, low probability of being asked out. You've seen how I sucked with *boy* <*space*> *friend* considering he was a friend to begin with. What more with first time acquaintances?

How bad am I? Once, I joined some friends for drinks. I rarely go to bars because I don't really drink, I don't like the noise and smoke, and I get sleepy easily. Guess what drink I ordered? A bottle of mineral water!

After a few minutes, a guy visiting from Liechtenstein took the seat beside me and struck a conversation. Later on, when his group was about to leave, he turned to me and said -

Hey, we're going to transfer to another bar. Want to join us?

I replied -

No, but thank you coz look at what I'm drinking... (as I pointed to my mineral water bottle to imply that I was a non-drinker)

Then he replied -

That's right and smart! Water first before alcohol to keep yourself hydrated.

He actually thought I was a boozer!

Here's another incident - one evening, a classmate from

business school messaged me online inviting me for a catch-up dinner because it had been years since we last saw each other. He also asked for my mobile number since he had trouble with his phonebook.

I just recently changed my mobile number and since I have not memorized my number yet, I saved my new number on my phone so I could easily copy and paste it when I needed to send it to contacts. I searched for it, then copied and pasted the number on the chat window.

My classmate replied back –

Just wondering but is it a coincidence we happen to have the same mobile number?

Apparently, it was his mobile number I copied and sent, not my mobile number!!! He must have thought I didn't want to share my number and I was sending a signal to talk to himself. But that wasn't my intention at all, believe me.

I am that bad at being asked out that I needed to step back and get the most basic dating tips from the most reliable sources - who else, but married friends - because they have gone through it and they have found their respective lifetime partners.

Their first tip was the usual - try to look great, dress up and put on some make-up. Unfortunately, I don't use make-up. I don't even own a lipstick. A tinted lip balm is the most sophisticated cosmetic product I own.

Then the second tip they gave me was something new (or maybe I was just ignorant that's why I was hearing it for the first time). They told me that if you were asked by the guy to pick the date place, choose a restaurant with warm white or soft white lights. Why? Because it hides all the imperfections of your skin and it would make your facial features look softer at any angle. (Please tell me you didn't also know this dating tip because otherwise it just validates my ignorance.)

My challenge with this tip though is that I don't like soft white lighting because I find it too dim. I feel safer when I see everything in natural color. Even my bedroom has bright white bulbs. I have no mood lights in my bedroom because the only moods I have at night are - mood for reading (lights on) and mood for sleeping (lights off). As for my facial features, nothing needs softening because I have chubby cheeks. They are at their softest from whichever angle and whatever light is available.

The last tip they gave me was I think customized for me. They told me to eat like a lady - at least on the first few dates. Yes, I eat like a man. But because I regularly exercise, my frame remains slim even with all the calorie intake.

As a rule of thumb, they say that the size of one's stomach equals a person's two fists put together and that should ideally be one's food consumption. Well, my food intake is more like the equivalent of my two fists ... times two! But hey, I have slim hands so maybe 4 fists' worth of food consumption isn't so bad.

One time, on a trip to Tokyo, there were 5 of us who had shabu-shabu and we finished 34 trays of meat, 10 trays of vegetables, 4 bowls of rice and 6 bowls of noodles. The group accused me of having the biggest appetite. But I defended myself and pointed the blame to another friend, but they all exclaimed –

But he is 6'3" and you're not!!!

Okay, I am just 5'6".

Another time, I attended a birthday lunch and I was seated beside a friend's friend. It was my first time to meet him. Before I got food from the buffet table, I warned my seatmate that I eat a lot. I usually disclose this to new acquaintances so I could freely eat to my heart's delight. This also gives them an opportunity to pre-judge me, so they won't be too preoccupied with shocking thoughts as they watch me devour food plateful after plateful.

After lunch, my seatmate told me –

When you said earlier that you eat a lot, I didn't think you were serious. Just don't do that on your first date.

Cringe.

And this explains why eating in moderation must be in the top 3 basic dating tips for me. Until I am certain that a guy is into me, I must eat a secret meal first before going out on a date.

But surprise, surprise - I bumped into my buffet seatmate a few months after the birthday lunch and guess what? He asked me out for a date even after giving me that cringe-inducing advice. At least I didn't have to eat a secret meal before our date.

*****

There's one unusual piece of advice I got from a married friend. She said to pretend to be a good cook even if you are not because men like women with good culinary skills. As the popular saying goes - *The way to a man's heart is through his stomach.*

This tip worked for her, she said. The guy, who eventually became her husband, only discovered the truth about her real culinary skills after they got married. But don't worry, she and her husband are still together and are happily married. My friend just hired a really good cook after they got married.

But here's the thing - I'm bad at lying. Plus, one lie could lead to another lie. If I cannot handle one lie, what more multiple ones?

So, I did a premortem exercise on this. If you're familiar with postmortem, premortem is its opposite. Postmortem is when you review something in hindsight or after it happened. Premortem is envisioning what could potentially go wrong or what will go wrong in advance.

Here's how my premortem exercise went –

If I were to lie about being a good cook, what if the guy asks next what my signature dish is? I must make another lie and name an impressive-sounding dish.

Then what if - out of curiosity - he asks me what are

the ingredients of the dish? So, I'll make another lie and rattle off a handful of ingredients I memorized or worse, I guessed.

Then what if - out of deep interest - he asks me how the dish is cooked? So, I'll make another lie and impress him with cooking terms like blanch, baste and dredge. This requires a lot of memorization which I am really bad at.

Then what if, one day, he asks me to cook my signature dish at his place (or my place)?! Ordering take-out food and transferring it to my own cookware so it looks like it was home-cooked will never work.

Doing this tactic of pretending to be a good cook may not work for me because I neither have the basic skills to pretend nor to memorize. Yes, I am so terrible in both memorization and acting ever since I was a kid.

When we were asked to recite an oral piece of our choice in junior high, do you know what piece I picked, aware of my limitations and capabilities? No, it was not Martin Luther King's *I Have a Dream*, nor Abraham Lincoln's *Gettysburg Address*, nor Winston Churchill's *We shall fight them on the beaches*, but all of these pieces were what most of my classmates performed. I picked a poem instead - something that didn't require drama and *uhm...* memorization.

I started my performance with a short introduction -

Unknown to many of us, what I am about to recite was actually a poem written in the early 19th century by a German priest named Joseph Mohr before it was given a melody by an Austrian named France Xaver Gruber.

A preamble to the oral piece was unnecessary but I had to justify what I was about to recite.

After such a build-up, the oral piece I recited was – *drum roll - Silent Night!*

There was another time when we were asked to recite a poem but since I already recited *Silent Night*, I had to find another piece. Fortunately, I found a poem with the same last line in all stanzas which means I had to memorize fewer lines. The poem was entitled "*Try, Try Again*" by T.H. Palmer.

But while I was practicing, I always got stuck at the fourth stanza. It seems the capacity of my brain for memorization is only up to 3 stanzas.

As backup, on the day of our recitation, I wrote the first line of the fourth stanza on my left palm so that if I forgot it, I could stealthily take a peek at it while I was making hand gestures.

I finally got called by the teacher. I began to recite -

Try, Try Again
by T.H. Palmer

'Tis a lesson you should heed,
If at first you don't succeed,
Try, try again;

Then your courage should appear,
For if you will persevere,
You will conquer, never fear
Try, try again;

Once or twice, though you should fail,
If you would at last prevail,
Try, try again;

If we strive, 'tis no disgrace
Though we do not win the race
What should you do in the case?
Try, try again.

Then WHAM! Suddenly, my mind went blank. I looked at the scribble on my palm, but it was the stanza I just recited! I couldn't remember the next line, so I looked at my teacher and said –

So sorry but I forgot the next line. Can I try again?

But guess what? The blunder actually worked in my favor. My teacher thought I did it on purpose because the poem was about trying again.

Anyway, so much for that. Now you get the point how terrible I am at memorization and acting. Pretending to be a good cook to impress guys may not work for me but I've heard of other real-life stories (other than my friend's testimony) where this has worked and it's not just on cooking skills.

For example, another friend told me about this story of a girl who pretended to like outdoor sports because the guy she was eyeing was into mountain-climbing. When the two were still dating, the girl joined all of the guy's hiking trips. After they got married, the girl didn't want to join any of the hiking trips anymore. Not sure what happened to them, but I just hope they worked it out even after the truth came out.

Then another real-life story was about this girl who liked a surfer dude, so she pretended to know how to surf (but take note, she has never surfed in her life, does not know how to swim and fears the open sea). The girl studied all the surfer terms so she can converse with the guy. One day, the surfer dude finally noticed her, and he asked her out on a date - to go surfing with him! The girl's plan was to fake an accident and show up on the date with a cast and crutches and to tell the guy that because of her injury, she cannot go surfing ever again. Sorry though, I don't know whatever happened on their first date. I haven't seen the person who told me this story since then. What a cliffhanger, I know.

Anyway, the crazy things people do for love! Maybe I need to be a little crazy for love too.

Plus One Plus None

4 NO PRESSURE

When I said I would take action when I was 33, I really did. I believed I did and not only was I taking action, but I was doing the best I can.

Except that before I knew it, a year went by and nothing different happened in my single life, but I told myself that the *new year* would be *"the year"*.

Except that before I knew it, 2 years went by and nothing different happened in my single life, but I told myself that the *new, new year* would be *"the year"*.

Except that before I knew it, 3 years went by and nothing different happened in my single life, but I told myself that the *new, new, new year* would be *"the year"*.

Except that before I knew it, 4 years went by ...

And before I knew it, I was already 37 and was still unmarried!!! *Hyperventilate.*

Where have all the years gone again?

Why does time fly so fast?

Why did nothing happen in the last 4 years?

Why haven't I met anyone yet?

Seriously, what was I doing wrong???

I had to figure this out if I seriously want to get married soon.

But wait, before you get the wrong impression, even if I was not married at 37, I have never complained about my single status. I was happy being single and I only realized this when one day, one of my nieces declared –

When I grow up, I don't want to get married. I want to be like Aunt Zita!

For the record, I have never said that I don't want to get married, so I don't know where my niece got that idea. When I asked why she wanted to stay unmarried like me, she said –

Because you have no problems and you're always happy.

Uh-oh.... She equated being happy and not having problems with being single. And she concluded from a sample size of one person - me.

The thing is, I am not even a reliable benchmark. I may be an outlier. For one, I grew up never being pressured to get married by my parents.

When I was in my teens and people asked my parents if I had a boyfriend, they replied –

Oh, she's still young...

When I graduated from university and people asked my parents if I had a boyfriend, my parents replied –

Oh, she's still young...

When I had a boyfriend and people asked my parents when my boyfriend and I would get married, they replied –

Oh, she's still young...

When my older brothers got married and people asked my parents when I would get married, they replied –

Oh, she's still young...

One day, I just realized my parents stopped saying –

Oh, she's still young...

When was the right time I wonder? At what point did I cross the young and not so young age? *Lol.*

So now you know why I only had my first boyfriend at 25. When your mind has been conditioned that you're young (even if you're not really young anymore) combined with introversion, you have one lethal combination. I suspect that if *boy <space> friend* was not that persistent, the accidental relationship would probably have never happened.

*****

My family not pressuring me to get married is probably an understatement. You could say that they are very supportive of my single status.

Once, an uncle was giving me a lecture on the many reasons I should get married and have my own family. His ultimate question was –

Who would take care of you when you grow old?

One of my brothers overheard my uncle and rushed to my side and he told my uncle –

Oh, we'll take care of our favorite sister.

Of course, I'm their favorite sister – I'm their only sister!

That topic did not end there. When my mom found out about my uncle's lecture, here's what my mom said –

Getting married and having kids is not a guarantee that someone will take care of you. I know of people with many kids but when they got old, not even one of their kids took care of them.

See, I don't even have to do any explaining. They are the ones doing all the rebuttal for me.

But wait, though I was happily single, I still wanted to get married because it's the path I knew as a kid - the linear storyline most of us expect to unfold in our lives - but I had to do some serious introspection and action because I was already 37.

Tick tock... Tick tock...

*****

So why did nothing happen in my single life in the last 4 years? There are many reasons but let's start with the simplest one - I am an introvert and being an introvert means:

- I don't enjoy small talk. I find small talk uncomfortable and sometimes even annoying.
- I attend parties to be there for loved ones when they celebrate milestones and special occasions (and okay, also for the food). Since I am not there to mingle and meet new people, I hang out with only the people I know during parties.
- When attending an event like a conference or a seminar, I like to stay at the back, by the wall, or near the exit. And I usually arrive when the event starts and leave a few minutes before it ends. This way, there is no room for small talk before and after the event.
- When a social obligation gets cancelled or rescheduled, or when I do not get invited to an event, especially if it's in the evening, I feel so relieved. Yes, I don't get offended at all if I don't get invited to parties, nor have any FOMO issues. My friends know that if ever they have to trim down their party guest list, they could automatically cross out my name. No questions asked.

In general, when I must interact with people, my energy easily gets sucked out. Just thinking about attending a social event where I don't know people too well (or don't know people at all) gives me butterflies in my stomach. I would rather be at home and alone.

But what do these have to do with my single status? It's not natural for me to meet new people, thus, limiting my chances of meeting prospects. And outside of work, I spend most of my time at home and alone.

On the rare occasions I go out socially, it's usually with the same set of friends.

Same set of friends 10 years ago...

15 years ago...

20 years ago ...

25 years ago...

30 years ago...

Yes, I still hang out with my friends from second grade

and added only a handful throughout the years.

How I wish I could tell you that the reason I am unenthusiastic about going out is that I live in a sleepy town or that I have to drive very far to reach the nearest restaurant or club. The thing is - I live in the central business district and right in my street are restaurants, cafes, and clubs. I have only to get out of my door, walk 12 steps to get to the elevator, push the button that says "G", then walk another 50 steps. That's all the effort I have to do to get to the nearest place where I could potentially meet people.

Or how I wish I could tell you that the reason for my dormant social life is because I am too old, and I no longer have the stamina to stay up late at night for gimmicks and parties. The latter part is actually true because when I am out, by around 10 pm, I already start yawning and getting sleepy. And you know what occupies my mind when I am out late at night? I think about all the people soundly sleeping in their beds and wish I were in my bed too. But here's the thing - for whatever unexplainable reason, when I am at home alone, I never run out of things to do and I am wide awake until 1 am, 2 am, 3 am…

Now you get the point - I love to stay at home alone. No excuses. No external factors beyond my control.

So earlier when I said I did real action and gave my best effort in the last 4 years, that is true in the context of being an introvert because every little effort to go out is uncomfortable, even painful, so I really believed that I was doing my best. But if you count the actual number of times I went out with someone (and I am too embarrassed to tell you how many!), they are numbers that won't move the needle.

Plus One Plus None

5 THE MATH

If your life revolves around the same set of people at work and the same circle of friends outside of work (yes, exactly my life!), what do you think are your chances of meeting your Plus One? It seems more like a solid plan to maximize your chances of having a Plus None.

And if you continue to coast along with this kind of life - *work, home, same friends, work, home, same friends* - before you know it, days turn into weeks, weeks turn into months, months turn into years, then you wonder -

Why haven't I found someone yet after all these years?

A better question to ask yourself is –

What did I do to find someone all these past years?

Yes, that was the question I had to answer honestly at 33 to solve the mystery of my dormant single life. I cannot expect someone to be knocking on my door if all I do is hope, pray, wish and wait. It's simple logic - no amount of praying, hoping and wishing can make anything happen if I spend most of my free time alone and at home.

Come to think of it, I don't even have food delivered at home. There's zero chance for anyone to even literally knock on my door.

*****

Albert Einstein once said –

Insanity is doing the same thing over and over again but expecting different results.

It is straight and simple logic but sometimes we are guilty of doing this, but we would not just admit it. In our heads, we would like to believe that we are doing something differently, but when you look closely and objectively assess, we are essentially doing the same thing but with just more effort.

More effort on doing the same thing is useless if that thing does not work in the first place. Thus, doing something differently is not just about working harder, or exerting more effort, or spending more time or doing your best. Rather, it is about identifying strategic solutions that could help you achieve the target results.

So okay, by Einstein's definition, I was insane in the last 4 years for believing I was exerting effort and doing my best and expecting that each year would be *"the year"* when I was not even doing anything differently.

*****

Since I do a lot of analysis at work, one day, I used my crude skills on analytics and forecasting for a better and more logical assessment of my situation and where my life was headed *"socially"* if I maintain my current trajectory. Shocking results.

If you want to go through the same exercise, please get a sheet of paper and pen. It's a quick exercise involving simple math.

Here goes:

How many Eligible Prospects (EPs) at an average do you meet in a week or a month? Multiply that by the number of weeks or months in a year to get the average number of Eligible Prospects (EPs) you meet in a year.

For someone to qualify as an Eligible Prospect (EP):
(1) You should have conversed with him.
(2) There is a way for you and the other person to contact each other, e.g. you have exchanged contact details, you have common friends or you can trace each other online; and
(3) He should be eligible and within your target age range.

If you cannot recall your EP numbers in the past weeks or months, let's use hypothetical figures for illustration purposes.

In a week, let's say you meet 1 new acquaintance at an average (regardless of age or gender).

In a year, that's 52 new acquaintances (as there are 52 weeks in a year).

But the thing is, not all of these 52 acquaintances are male and eligible, thus, we must make certain percentage assumptions. For easy math, let's just assume that 5 out of every 10 new people you meet (or 50%) are male. Then among these males, 1 out of every 10 (or 10%) are eligible (uncommitted and within your target age range).

Therefore:
1 new acquaintance per week
x 52 weeks
x 50% male
x 10% eligible
= 2.6 EPs

That means out of the 52 new acquaintances you meet in a year, only 2 to 3 of them would qualify as Eligible Prospects. Yes, that's all for one entire year.

I just want to remind you these figures are purely hypothetical. For better accuracy and reliability, you must use your own sample data. You can monitor how you do in the next 4 weeks so you can use your actual one-month snapshot to estimate your annual numbers. In simplest terms, the Eligible Prospects (EP) formula is:

> Average no. of new acquaintances you meet in a week
> x 52 weeks
> x % split of your target gender
> x % eligibility rate
> = Eligible Prospects (EPs) in a year

Simple math, right?

If you're not happy with your annual numbers, don't fret. There is hope - at least conceptually. This time, I will use my rudimentary skills on optimization to improve the numbers.

What does optimization mean? Optimization is about being more strategic with your actions by focusing on the variables that matter most so your numbers keep on improving.

Which variables can be optimized? It could be any one variable, a combination, or all of the following variables:

- average number of new acquaintances per week
- gender split ratio
- eligibility rate

By increasing any one of these variables, any two, or all three, you'll have higher EPs in a year.

For illustration, let's say you optimized the average number of new acquaintances you meet in a week by joining a professional organization where you've committed to meet at least 2 new members weekly. Using the EP formula, let's re-compute and plug in 2 new people per week but all the other assumptions remain the same.

> Therefore:
> 2 new acquaintances per week
> x 52 weeks
> x 50% male
> x 10% eligibility rate

= 5.2 EPs in a year

Your annual EPs doubled by just optimizing one variable. But let's say you're still not happy with 5 EPs in a year because you're too picky, thus, there may be a slim chance your special someone could be 1 out of 5 EPs. There's also a chance that none of the 5 EPs might be into you, right? Time to further optimize.

To improve your numbers, maybe you decided to swap the professional organization with clubs related to your personal interests like a tech org and a diving club where members are mostly male and within your target age group. You still committed to meet 2 new members per week, but the gender split now is more male, and the eligibility rate is higher because most members are within your target age range. This time you're able to optimize 2 more variables - the gender ratio and eligibility rate. Below are your new assumptions:

- meet 2 new people in a week
- new gender split of 65% male (versus 50% in the previous example)
- new eligibility rate of 20% (versus 10% in the previous example)

To compute:
2 new acquaintances in a week
x 52 weeks
x 65% male
x 20% eligibility rate
= 13.52 EPs in a year

Such a big jump in EPs compared to when you only optimized one variable.

As you can see from these hypothetical illustrations, by creating opportunities to meet more new people, or by focusing on activities where you can meet many people within your target age group or within your target criteria in one go, you'll be able to keep on improving your EP numbers.

All these are based on simple logic - you must interact with people if you want to increase your chances of meeting your potential partner. If you do not make yourself available out there, people won't know you exist.

Since I am an introvert, when I did this exercise at 33, my assumptions were based on the capacity and capabilities of an introvert. I am not at all strategic in my ways to meet EPs because most of the "*new people*" I meet are out of my target age range. (Translation — "*kids*" - when I attend children's parties of my friends' kids. *Lol.*)

At work, I am able to put into good use my analytics, forecasting and optimization skills but when it comes to my single status situation, unfortunately, I am only good at theory but suck at execution. If I really, really want to open my doors to the possibility of having a Plus One and not ending up with a Plus None, I seriously have to go out of my comfort zone.

Again, the objective of this exercise is to quickly assess your current situation and get some indicative numbers if you actually get to meet EPs assuming you just coast along your current life. If your numbers are alarming, you definitely must take action because if you do nothing differently and you don't make improvements consistently, then nothing new would most likely happen in your single life. Years from now, just like in the past years, you would still find yourself not far from where you are now - still single, only older — yes, exactly like what happened in my life in the last 4 years.

6 OCCASIONS AND BLIND DATES

Even after knowing that my annual EP numbers suck, I wasn't gung-ho about joining organizations or engaging in activities to meet new people. I was only willing to do baby steps even if at my age, what I needed was a quantum leap.

Again, I am taking full accountability. There is no one else to blame but myself if my efforts are so puny and so slow that they make no impact.

So what baby steps was I willing to do? A lot of my married friends say that occasions are a great way to meet people. I have heard about couples who first met at weddings, baptisms and birthday parties. But guess what? I have been a bridesmaid in 13 weddings and have been a godmother in 27 baptismal ceremonies, but I have not met anyone from these occasions whom I ended up going out with. But then again, I didn't really socialize in those events because I always made a French exit after eating.

In some occasions where I stayed longer, I unfortunately ended up making a fool of myself like in this wedding where I was a bridesmaid and I had to participate in the bridal bouquet toss.

Being an introvert, the bouquet toss is my dreaded part

of the wedding reception, so I usually escape by going to the toilet or staying in the lounge until it's over. But since I was a bridesmaid, I couldn't escape because participation was mandatory. To make it worse, it wasn't the traditional bouquet toss where I can easily pretend I am positioned to catch the bouquet but never actually move once it's tossed. Instead, the rule of this bouquet toss was that the bride would throw individual flowers one at a time and the girl who doesn't catch any flower will be "it" and she will be paired with the groom's "it". Together, they would play a couple's game with the newlyweds in front of all the guests. *Shiver*.

I had to catch a flower. Being "it" was not an option.

What happened?

First flower thrown - I missed it.

Second flower thrown - I missed it again.

Third flower thrown - I missed it again. *Argggh...*

Fourth flower thrown - I missed it again. *Panic.*

Fifth flower thrown - I grabbed the flower but another girl grabbed the stem. We both didn't want to let go of what we were holding so it was split into two. I got the flower and she got the stem.

I wasn't sure if a flower without a stem would spare me from being "it" so to be sure, I was determined to catch another flower.

When I saw that there were only a handful of flowers left for my bride friend to throw, I gave it my all in a last-ditch attempt to secure another flower. I felt the sudden surge of adrenaline course through my veins and I dove to catch a flower and *BOOM!* I landed on the floor. Goodbye, dignity and poise. But yes, I successfully caught a complete flower.

Finally, the tossing of flowers stopped. The host announced that the game was intended to allow each of us to catch a flower. We were tricked! Then the host explained that the flowers had stems of varying lengths and the girl who caught the flower with the shortest stem was "it". *Uh-oh.* I had two flowers all right - one had no stem at all and the other one had a stem which was ... 2 centimeters long! I was "it".

Maybe it was high time for me to level up when attending occasions, to commit to being more proactive in making new friends, to stick around a little longer after eating, and hopefully, to not to make a fool of myself.

*****

Something unsettles me though when I attend special occasions - the intrusive small talk with strangers. This doesn't just happen to singles but to anyone regardless of one's status.

The intrusion starts with the basic small talk question - *Are you single or married?* Then depending on one's answer, it could lead to any of these follow-up questions:

If you're single: *Do you have a boyfriend?*
If yes> *When are you getting married?*
If no> *Why don't you have a boyfriend?*

If you're married: *Do you have kids?*
If yes> *When do you plan to have your next baby?*
If no> *Why don't you have kids yet?*

If you're separated: *Why? What happened?*
If you're a single parent: *Why? What happened?*

It just goes on and on...

Personally, I find these questions a bit sensitive especially if you are asking random strangers.

What if the single lady you asked just had a really bad breakup and is depressed?

What if the married couple you asked had been trying to have a baby in the last 5 years?

What if the married woman you asked just had a

miscarriage?

What if the married man you asked just discovered that his wife was cheating on him?

I know most people have no malicious intentions when they ask these questions but if you want to make small talk, there are a lot of other topics to talk about without making someone feel uncomfortable.

*****

For single ladies, besides one's civil status, the other unnerving question is – *How old are you?*

When you are in your early twenties, the age question is not a problem. In fact, you are most likely to seek other people's age out of curiosity and even volunteer your age.

When you hit 25, it's still no problem. You are still probably one of the youngest in the workplace.

When you hit 28 or 29, that's the time you realize that you are not that young anymore as you notice newer and younger people in the workplace.

I bet the first time you realized this was when you were about to turn 30. Perhaps, one lunch break, upon realizing that you were approaching your thirties, you exclaimed loudly -

Oh no, I am so old already! I'm almost 30!

Suddenly, you noticed that some of your colleagues are throwing dagger looks at you. Then it hit you - some are in their 30s, 40s, and 50s. *Uh-oh*. If you consider 30 as old already, what does that make the rest of them? Or shall I say, the rest of us?

*****

Have you ever noticed that usually, the civil status and age questions go together? Either the civil status question is asked first followed by the age question such as –

Interrogator: *Are you single or married?*
Me: *Single*
Interrogator: *How old are you?*
Me: *37*
Interrogator: *What?! How can you still be single???*

If you're still young, it should be an easy conversation as the interrogator would say something like – *Oh, you're still young. You still have a lot of time to date and meet people.*

At other times, the age question is asked first followed by the civil status question such as –
Interrogator: *How old are you?*
Me: *37*
Interrogator: *You must be married. So how many kids do you have?*
Me: *No, I'm still single.*
Interrogator: *What?! Why aren't you married yet?*

There is no way out whether the interrogator asks the age question first or the civil status question first.
So, how do I deal with it when a stranger asks me –
"*How old are you*"?
I simply answer back –
How old do you think am I?
And whatever the other person guesses (which is usually younger than my real age), I reply –
Wow, you're really good! You guessed it right!

*****

Speaking of age-related questions, here are two funny anecdotes.

One time, a friend set me up for a blind date with a colleague. My friend told her colleague that the two of us were middle school classmates and long-time friends. Then her colleague suddenly asked her –
May I know how old is your friend?

My friend didn't want to answer the question because if she answers it, it would reveal her age too because after all, she told the guy we were classmates. Guess what she replied to the guy?

Oh, she's our age!

Yes, she said that even if she didn't know the guy's age. And yes, I dated someone who I had no idea what his age was, but I'll tell you more about this date later.

Then once on a trip to Bangalore, I was chatting with the hotel car driver while caught in heavy traffic. In our conversation, I discovered that his marriage was arranged. He only met his bride-to-be a few months before the wedding. For us who do not have such a tradition, it's unthinkable to be subjected to it. Imagine not having the freedom to choose your lifetime partner?

Out of curiosity, I asked him if he or any of his friends thought about running away right before their weddings. He replied –

No, no, no, as he bobbled his head.

No one runs away. Our elders know us best. They raised us, they saw us grow up, and they know our values, character, strengths, and weaknesses. They know what makes us happy, sad and angry. They are in the best position to find our perfect match. We obey and respect their decisions.

Awww... what a beautiful answer! And yes, his arranged marriage worked, and it was going strong.

Then I asked at what age do girls and boys usually get subjected to an arranged marriage. He said that for boys, the age doesn't really matter but it's really more for girls because of their biological clock. He said –

For me, when I was in the marrying age, I was okay to marry someone between 18 years old up to .... <long pause as he thought deeply> *... maybe 25 years old...*

Then he paused again to reflect on what he just said, and he continued -

Yes, I think 25 years old is the oldest age of a girl I would consider marrying... beyond 25 is already too old for me, as he bobbled his head again.

Then we talked about his wedding, his wife, his kids, his parents, his parents-in-law, his cows... then suddenly, he remembered to ask me the civil status and age questions!

He asked -
How about you? Are you married?
I replied -
No. I'm not married yet.
Then he asked -
If you don't mind, may I know how old are you?
I replied -
How old do you think am I?
He answered -
25???

Of course, I don't look 25 at all! He was just being polite. He just rattled off the maximum acceptable age he considered "still young" from our earlier conversation. *Lol.*

*****

Given my poor dating skills, my dismal statistics, my spotty track record, my puny efforts, and my snail pace, I could already predict that it would be a long and uneventful dating life for me.

If I really want to have real dates, I had to accept that I needed external help, otherwise, my dates will all be solo dates. Not that I am complaining because remember, I enjoy being alone. But hey, if I really want to have a Plus One, I had to get out of my comfort zone by being more open to blind dates especially if I cannot meet new people on my own.

I've to admit that when I was in my twenties, I wasn't that open to being set up for blind dates because when you're in your twenties, you feel like you have all the time in the world and there are so many single people out there.

There is nothing to worry about, nothing to rush. And you think it should be easy to mingle and find a lot of EPs when you are ready to commit.

But when you hit your thirties, most people you meet either have girlfriends, or are married, or have other gender preferences. You realize that EPs are getting scarcer and scarcer.

If I really want to get things going given that I have a low ability (or worse, no ability) to generate EPs on my own, I must get external help and be open to being set up for blind dates.

The big problem was - blind dates make me feel awkward and really, really nervous. I get anxious just thinking about having a conversation over a meal with a stranger. Sometimes, I even secretly hope that something crops up last minute so the date gets postponed. I know I sound so weird but that's how weird I am which I am trying to change and improve on.

Are you ready to hear some of my blind date anecdotes?

For some preamble, let me first describe to you my social media usage. I have social media accounts, but I don't post any content. My last post was a profile photo update. When? Five years ago.

I used to occasionally post content but when people comment or post questions, I feel that out of courtesy, I must respond. I don't want to respond because other than it's time-consuming, whatever I shared in a post, that's everything I want to share. No more, no less.

I don't check social media feeds either because if you do, before you know it, you've spent three hours mindlessly browsing through random posts.

Why do I even have social media accounts in the first place? For private messaging and for work such as managing business pages. That's it.

But what does social media have to do with my blind date efforts? Social media is a good source to find out more about your prospective date. But since it's not my behavior to stalk online (partly because I don't want to form any biases before meeting someone), I usually never know how my blind date looks like. I didn't realize there was merit to online stalking to at least get an idea on how a person looks like until one blind date experience.

This blind date and I agreed to meet in a coffee shop. He arrived first and messaged me he was by the bookshelves and that he was wearing a shirt with blue stripes. When I reached the place, surprise, surprise - there were three guys dining alone and they all were wearing blue-striped shirts!

Another struggle for me when I am out on a blind date is doing small talk. You grapple for topics to find common interests interspersed with gaps of awkward silence. If nothing seems to be common except for the friend who hooked you up, guess what? You'll end up talking about your common friend. By the end of the night, you know more about your friend than your date.

Why can't there be a more natural way to meet guys? In movies, it always happens. In real life, scenes aren't as perfect and polished. Most of the time, they are awkward and embarrassing. But what I learned as I became older was that embarrassment won't kill you. You just must learn how to suck it all in and laugh at yourself like what happened to me on one blind date.

For some context, the guy and I are within the same age range. I usually ask for an indicative age of my date from the person setting us up just to make sure the guy and I are always within the same age range. I'm very traditional and old fashioned this way - I still prefer someone within my age group or older.

Anyway, while we were out, my blind date saw a girl he used to go out with. I told him that the girl looks stunning and I asked him why he stopped seeing her. He answered —

Oh, I don't date young girls anymore. I prefer more mature ones.

I asked -
What do you mean by "more mature"?
He replied -
Somewhere between 25 to 28 years old.

Lol. That moment seemed both comical and surreal for me. My raw thoughts were –

Does this guy actually know how old I am? If yes, is he that tactless? If no, did he actually think I was in my mid-twenties? Either way, I could not believe it. I just laughed it off because if the guy did not honestly know my age, at least he would not feel embarrassed about what he just said. Oh well, that's what I got for asking an unnecessary question.

Surprisingly, he asked me out again for a second and a third date, but I had to decline his invitations after that because I didn't think we have the same wavelength. It was draining for me to carry out conversations where I cannot intellectually connect with a person. And for sure, once he discovers that I'm nowhere near 25 to 28 years old, he'll also be out in a flash.

*****

I just remembered the one exemption among my blind dates whose age I didn't know. Remember my classmate who didn't want to reveal her age to her colleague? She told me that based on the guy's looks, she sincerely thought we were all of the same age that's why she set us up. I trusted my friend's judgment and went out with the guy.

What happened? During our conversation, I deduced the guy's age because he would give bits and pieces of information about his career such as he worked in so-so company for xx years and in so-so company for xx years, etc. My brain automatically computed his indicative age based on his total years of work experience. He was 6 years younger than me!

Other than being younger, my brain automatically assessed too that he wasn't my type. Therefore, I had to do something during dinner so he won't take an interest in me. Since he loved to talk about his career, I encouraged him to talk more about it so I don't have to talk about myself. I also gave him career advice like pursuing his dream job since I had more wisdom than him, after all I was 6 years older.

Do you know what feedback he told my friend the following day? He said that our date was like a career counseling session and that I would make a great HR person. *Lol*.

And guess what? Three months after our date, he left for Maldives to pursue his dream job.

*****

After several blind dates, I realized I was doing something wrong. While a date is ongoing, my mind is automatically processing and assessing if the two of us would click or not based on our initial conversation. If not, I would start shutting down and the more I would not open up. Everything goes downhill from there.

And so, I reflected - how come when I go out on a date, my mind goes into automatic assessment mode?

Then I realized two things:

#1 - Immediately after a first date, friends excitedly ask you if you think your date is The One (or not). It's as if you are expected to give a verdict after just one meeting.

But what I realized was - I am not at all obliged to give them a verdict, not even after the second or third date. I don't even have to answer their questions in the first place (though this comes with a potential risk that some would start unfriending me). But then again, no one has to know that I'm going out on a date except the one setting me up. If no one knows, then no one would ask questions, ergo, I've nothing to declare.

#2 - I am too left-brained. When my head says we're not a good match based on our values, interests and the way we connect in conversations, or when he's out of my target age range, I see it as a waste of time if I would still continue seeing the person. If I know that I'm not that into him but it seems like he's into me, I would rather cut it short as I don't want to mislead him or give him false expectations.

Given the two realizations above, perhaps my biggest flaw for dating is - I have the wrong mindset. For example - who wouldn't be nervous or uncomfortable on the first date, especially on a blind date, right? Even on the second or third date, you would probably be still shy, reserved, or not be your usual self.

If you ask any of your married friends too, chances are, most would tell you they saw dating as a fun way to make new friends. They developed friendships with their dates even if they weren't their type. And yes, they went out with them again, not just once or twice but several times. Some even became good friends after realizing they weren't meant to be. Some eventually ended up together as a couple. And for some others, by a funny twist of fate, they have met their lifetime partners through past dates who introduced them to the person they eventually married.

*****

After my big realizations about dating, I had to re-wire my brain.

Dating is not about pressuring yourself to decide right after the first date if you could potentially like or not like a person in a special way. Instead, dating is about making new friends. So, what if the person isn't your type? He could still be a potential friend. But to develop friendships, you must try to open up - yes, even if you are an introvert.

Game on! Zita 2.0 is ready to date again.

One sunny day, a friend called me. She had a blind date for me. Yay! I could finally put into practice my learnings.

The day of reckoning finally arrived. During the first few minutes of my dinner date, my mind automatically processed and assessed my date again! *Argghhh*... How do I turn off this *my type/not my type* detector when I go out on dates?

Sadly, the guy wasn't my type but guess what? I did it! I was actively engaged in our conversation throughout the night. I also kept my evasion tactics to minimum when he asked me some personal questions.

I would like to think that the date went well because he asked me out again except that I was busy.

And he messaged me regularly.

Then he asked me out again except that I was busy again...

He still continued to message me regularly.

Then he asked me out again, but I was still busy ...

Until one day, the messages and invitations just stopped.

Uh-oh.

What's the learning here? I didn't make time for him and I didn't try hard enough to develop the friendship.

After he stopped messaging and inviting me, I made no effort to reconnect with him because it was during a time when I was really busy at work. All my free time was reserved to catch up on sleep. Although I've to admit, that if he were my type, I am sure I would have exhausted all efforts to accept his invitations even if it meant giving up precious sleeping hours or even being absent from work. As the cliché goes, *when there's a will, there's a way*.

Anyway, life moved on after that episode. Fast forward to 5 months.

One day, I got a call from the same friend who set me up with the guy. But my friend called me to ask about something else.

At the end of our long conversation, she asked -
Hey, how's Josh?
I said -
Huh? Sorry, who is Josh?
My friend replied -
Your blind date - the guy I set you up with a few months back.
Shiver.

I felt my blood draining from my face. I thought the guy's name was Mark the entire time!!!

I quickly checked my phonebook - he was saved as Mark!

I checked my outbox - I addressed him as Mark in all my messages!

How could have that happened???!!! The names "Josh" and "Mark" have nothing in common - not even a single letter. The guy must have thought I was such a player dating a lot of men!

7 ONLINE DATING

My last dating blunder was really embarrassing. It's still a mystery to me how I could have possibly gotten the guy's name wrong because before I started actively going out on blind dates, I re-read some parts of Dale Carnegie's *How to Win Friends and Influence People*, a favorite book of my dad.

Ever since I became a young adult, my dad would bug me to read this book every summer - perhaps to make sure I could really make friends. But I've to admit that I have never read the book from cover to cover. I just usually read the part about remembering people's names because my dad used to tell me that if there's one key takeaway to remember from the book, it had to be that *a person's name is like music to one's ears.*

To bring my learning one notch higher, I applied another lesson from the book - that of repetition. When conversing with someone, the key is to repeat the person's name every now and then. This way, the name would easily stick to your memory while you are bringing music to someone's ears. Win-win, right?

Following such advice, can you imagine how my messages to Josh were peppered with the wrong name??? That's how bad and embarrassing the Josh episode was!

Instead of bringing music to his ears, I probably made him cringe every time I called him Mark. But nope, he never corrected me in any of those times. Maybe he was too embarrassed for me.

*****

Am I that hopeless when it comes to dating? Are there other ways I can meet people if I cannot pull it off on blind dates?

Some friends suggested online dating. I know of some people who met their partners online and eventually got married. Could it be a viable option for me? But I have issues and fears about online dating such as:

- I feel uncomfortable uploading my photos online. Once uploaded, you can never truly control what happens to them as anyone can easily download or take screenshots.

- I don't know what to put in my description. Is there something interesting I can write about myself? Or are my interests only interesting to me?

- What if someone I know sees my profile?

- What if I get matched with someone I know?

- What if the guy I am corresponding with is a psychopath? Or a con artist? Or a criminal?

- What if we really connect online but when we meet in person, we do not click?

- What if he lives across the globe? Am I capable of having a long-distance relationship?

- What if we madly fall in love? Will I move to another country or continent to be with him?

Am I open to relocating if it takes that to make it work? That's a good question because honestly, I don't.

I have been to a lot of beautiful places, but not once have I pictured myself living in any of those places. I could picture myself living in some of them for a few months but definitely not permanently moving. I am happy in the small spot I occupy on Earth where I am close to family and friends.

In the past, I have even turned down career opportunities in some of the most exciting cities in the world just to stay in my happy spot. I have never considered relocating for career or money, but will I do it for love? Or am I that risk averse that I would always opt to stay in my guaranteed happy spot?

It's so selfish of me and I am fully aware of this. I am where I am - still single - because I do not want to give up a lot of things.

But despite all these uncertainties, I still decided to give online dating a try for 5 reasons:

1. All the people I know who found their partners online are still happily married. Looks promising.

2. If I don't do something new to meet eligible prospects (given that I failed big time in blind dates), how do I expect to have different results? So, this is something new I could do and see if it produces the target results.

3. If my Plus One is from across the globe, maybe he could be the one who would move to my happy spot, not vice-versa.

4. With online dating, I can get to know a person virtually first, then decide if I want to go on a face-to-face date. That's a very efficient way to filter out unsuitable prospects without causing unnecessary anxiety especially if the guy isn't my type.

5. There is no way I could get a person's name wrong in online dating because the name of the guy I am chatting with will always be on the screen.

*****

So, I did online dating. Let me describe to you how my profile looked. This was the most I was willing to do.

I uploaded 3 photos.

Photo # 1 - It was a full body shot taken from a

distance.

Photo # 2 - It was a half-body shot but I was wearing dark sunglasses.

Photo # 3 - No dark sunglasses but it was a side view shot.

I decreased the resolution of the photos so that if someone pinches to zoom in, they become pixelized. This way, if someone who knows me sees my photos, he won't be sure if it's me or just someone who looks like me.

Then my description read –

Bookworm, technophile, philomath and phytophilous.

I just realized now how geeky my profile sounded.

Then I used a pseudonym which sounded more like a droid's name. Think R2-D2 and C-3PO.

I know. Everything about my profile screams BORING. The results? Only a handful of matches contacted me. And I am sharing these with you so you could do the total opposite if you want to try online dating. This serves as your quick what-not-to-do guide when you create your online dating profile.

You're welcome.

*****

Given my boring online dating profile, only a handful of prospects contacted me and I responded to most even if I didn't really think our profiles or interests were a good fit. I had to force myself to do this because I had to be more open, remember?

Out of all these prospects, there was this one person who consistently sent me messages. He was officially my first match shortly after signing up. He didn't seem like a psychopath. The topics we talked about were normal and safe topics like movies, TV shows, hobbies, weekend activities... nothing too serious or intrusive.

Yes, in online dating, you will encounter some matches who would immediately ask you very personal, intrusive, and sometimes shocking questions ranging from past relationships, views about marriage, how affectionate you are, your personal hygiene habits and even your sleeping habits.

So, going back to this first match, he was located across the globe. We had opposite time zones. He was a single dad and has a 6-year old daughter. His daughter stays with him on weekends and she stays with the mom on weekdays. Red flag. That means if we fall in love, he cannot relocate to my happy spot.

Anyway, he consistently messaged me every day until one day, over a long holiday, he went on a skiing trip. I never heard from him since then. He just stopped messaging. He ghosted on me.

Maybe something bad happened to him?

Maybe he found another match more interesting?

Maybe he gave up on me because every time he asked if we could already exchange personal contact details and do a video call, I kept on declining and insisted that we should stick to chatting within the app first?

But whatever the reason is, I was relieved that my correspondence with ski guy stopped because I did not see where it would go – again, because of the relocation issue. I think I must overcome my personal issues first and be more open to the possibility of relocating if I want online dating to work for me.

The problem with me is when I could somehow see where something is headed and I don't really like the potential outcome and/or the available options, I'd rather stop immediately. This is one of my many peculiarities and another reason I am still single. Told you, I am fully accountable for my single status.

If you find yourself complaining why you still don't have a boyfriend or why your dating efforts aren't working, you must do a tough love self-assessment. Maybe it's not about them but it's about you. Maybe just like me, you have made a lot of self-imposed restrictions that limit your options and bring down the number of your prospects to almost nil.

*****

Did anything ever pan out from my online dating efforts after ski guy? Zilch.

As for the other matches, I replied to most, but I stopped replying to those who insisted on exchanging contact details too soon or those who asked inappropriate or creepy questions.

But I also did something out of my comfort zone and out of character. I proactively contacted some guys whose profiles I found interesting. Yes, I mustered the guts to do the first move except that no one responded! *Lol.* I could not really blame them for ignoring me given my low-res profile photos, geeky description and my droid-sounding name. I am sure they already concluded that I was dull and boring.

More key takeaways from online dating:

- It's totally okay if some matches reject you because you would reject some too.

- If you see a match with profile photos and a dull description (similar to mine), please do not immediately judge the person. Maybe, just maybe, the person is shy, reserved and very private (like me).

*****

I don't know if I was overly cautious with my attempt at online dating, but I really could not help it because we're talking about interacting with total strangers. Who knows if some are just using other people's photos and fake identities?

Plus, when I researched online dating, I discovered that online dating scams are so prevalent. I was so shocked and horrified by the stories.

Scammers have a playbook to manipulate victims and even the most rational person could fall into the trap because the tactics used are based on psychological principles, thus, everything sounds and feels so real.

Here are some of the common patterns I noticed from the scam stories I read (if you are considering online dating):

- Scammers target older people (likely to have more savings), and widows and widowers (likely to have gotten some inheritance from the deceased spouse).

- Scammers usually have sad life stories such as their parents are both deceased, and they have no siblings which means they have no living immediate family member. They also usually claim they have an ex-partner or a stepparent or a relative who is physically abusive and that's why they have no social media accounts for fear of being tracked by the abuser. Such stories are a sure way to elicit one's compassion and nurturing side. There is another purpose why scammers choose such personal backgrounds. With no immediate family member or social media account in existence, there is no way to verify the scammer's true identity.

- Scammers would suggest exchanging personal contact details shortly after a couple of chat sessions. This is the reason I filtered out the ones who requested contact details too soon as this could be a red flag. I think it's okay to exchange contact details once you have gauged that the other person seems trustworthy and his answers are plausible and consistent. But until then, the getting-to-know-you stage must be via the dating app.

- Immediately after the scammer and victim have some kind of mutual understanding, scammers usually suggest that they both close their dating accounts since they have found each other already. This is to make sure that the victim never discovers that the scammer's account remains active on the dating platform.

- Calls are almost always initiated by the scammer and

they are usually one-way video calls - the scammer sees the victim on video, but the victim never sees the scammer because only the scammer's computer audio or phone audio works. The scammer's usual excuse is that his webcam or his mobile phone's camera is busted. But what is the real reason? The scammer used fake photos so he is a different person as the one in the profile photos that's why he cannot show himself on live video.

- To prove their trust for each other, scammers would request the victims' social media account passwords. If a victim is hesitant to share her password, the scammer would insinuate that maybe she does not trust him yet or there are pieces of content in her social media accounts which she wants to hide from him. I know it is super crazy to give passwords away but because the victims are under some kind of love trance, they willingly give their passwords away out of blind trust. Shortly after, a fake account of the victim emerges. But even with the sudden emergence of a fake account, victims usually never suspect that their online soulmates did it. Instead, they conclude that their accounts were simply hacked.

- When scammers call, they usually call victims at odd hours to tell the victim about their problems and emergencies. This deprives the victim of proper sleep so one cannot think clearly especially when the scammer asks for money. Yes, they ask for money for various creative reasons such as they were traveling and got robbed and don't have money to buy a return ticket, someone in the family must urgently undergo a major surgery, their credit card was hacked and they have no other card to use for an urgent expense, etc.

These are some of the things I could remember from the horror stories I have read online but please, also do your own research as scam tactics evolve.

Here's the saddest part though - because victims have been psychologically manipulated and have been blinded by love, all requests for money (medical emergency, family emergency, financial loss in a business, physical threat, personal accident, legal problems, airfare, tuition fees, etc.) always seem real so the victims usually send money each and every time - even if the requests come one after another. Unfortunately, the victims rarely share such details with their family and friends until they realize their financial losses are so huge, or there is nothing more to send, or they are already being blackmailed by the scammers.

The scam stories are really heartbreaking. It's one thing that the victims have been emotionally duped and it's another that they have been financially swindled. Some victims have even lost their entire life savings to scammers.

Knowing about all these scam tactics was one reason why I was so paranoid and overly cautious when I tried online dating. As a precaution before I signed up to dating platforms, I told a friend that if one day I tell her I have met my soulmate online but have never met him face-to-face yet nor had a video call with him yet, she has to punch me, scream at me, embarrass me, hit me hard on the head, and exhaust all possible means to bring me back to my senses.

But then again, maybe that would never happen to me because when the scammer profiles me, he would know that if he ever asks for money, I would never lend him money but instead give him a whole slew of solutions and a worksheet that shows all the comparative rates and payment terms.

8 DEAR GOD

Have you ever made a list of the traits of your ideal partner? If you did, have you noticed how your list changed as you grew older? In my case, this evolution was evident in my prayer for a Plus One.

Below are some of my prayer versions but please note that the traits are in no particular order. I just numbered the criteria for easy reference so you could see the transition from one version to another.

Version 1 went like this:

Dear God,
Please give me someone who -
1. is kind
2. has a great sense of humor
3. is God-fearing
4. diligently goes to mass
5. is respectful to elders
6. is close to his family
7. loves kids
8. treats people nicely regardless of one's status
9. has good character
10. shares the same values I have

11. is hard-working
12. is smart
13. has clear goals in life
14. doesn't smoke
15. doesn't drink
16. doesn't have dogs or pets (I am generally scared of animals except for fish pets - I'm good with that)
17. is good-looking
18. is financially stable
19. is taller than me.
Amen.

I know it's a long list. It was my original list of non-negotiables when I was in my 20s because as they say, if you're going to ask God or wish for something, you might as well ask for the best. ☺

During this period, there was a time when I went out with someone who lives just a couple of blocks away from the church where I attend mass and I excitedly asked –

So, do you also hear mass at XX church?

He replied -

Yes, every Christmas!

Uh-oh... He goes to mass only once a year! Criteria #4 - Fail. Other than that, there were also some other mismatched values, but I started really zoning out right after learning about his mass attendance.

Date after date, the same thing happened. I would uncover some things about my date where he falls short, and because of that, I don't want to go out on a second date anymore. Clearly, my prayer version 1 wasn't working. Maybe my filters were too much.

By Version 4, my prayer went like this:

Dear God,
Please give me someone who -
1. is kind
2. has a great sense of humor

3. is God-fearing
4. treats people nicely regardless of one's status
5. has good character
6. shares the same values I have
7. has clear goals in life
8. doesn't smoke
9. (preferably) doesn't drink or occasionally drinks only
10. is financially stable.
It would be a great bonus if he's taller than me and if he's cute. Amen.

Yes, filters were slashed by almost half! And if you've noticed, good looks and height became just optional. I know these are superficial traits so shame on me for being too shallow when I was younger.

Sadly, version 4 still didn't work.
Fast forward to Version 8. It went like this:

Dear God,
Please give me someone who -
1. is God-fearing
2. treats people kindly
3. has good family values
4. makes me laugh
5. is financially responsible
And it would be a great bonus if he is pleasing to my eyes (after all, beauty is in the eyes of the beholder). Amen.

Version 8 was just one-fourth of my original list. Totally goodbye to good looks and height even if they were only optional in v4.

But sadly, even the trimmed down Version 8 still didn't work.

Version 12 went like this:

Dear God,

Please give me someone who is God-fearing, responsible and kind (kind to everyone and not just to me and our loved ones). Amen.

It was down to the bare minimum - the core essentials. Maybe this was a sign of maturity.

How I wish though I could tell you that Version 12 was "it". It still wasn't the case.

I realized that maybe I wasn't praying the right way... or maybe I did not know how to listen to God. I had to radically change how I prayed.

So, Version 16 went like this:

Dear God,
When you finally make us meet, can you please make me realize that it's him? And just in case he's already in my life now and I am too clueless and dense to realize it, please give him the patience to persevere until I recognize it's him. Amen.

Version 16 was actually my way of telling God - "*Thy will be done*" but God has to make me realize when it happens because I might not be aware that it is happening already.

Version 16 also happens to be my final prayer version not because it finally worked, but I stopped praying it after the Mark/Josh blooper.

Why did I stop praying it? Because I realized that if I were dead serious and sincere about my prayer, how come I could not even get a person's name right? I bug God every night about giving me someone but when he sends a prospect my way, I could not even remember basic details. How can God help me if I am not helping myself and doing my part?

But hey, I still pray every night, but I pray for a lot of other prayer petitions. In the grand scheme of things, my prayer petition is not that important anyway. I realized this when one time I went on a pilgrimage to the Basilica of Our Lady of Lourdes in France which is known for many miracles. I was praying for my usual personal petitions including finding my Plus One when suddenly, I realized that I was surrounded by people fighting for their lives - people terminally sick, in stretchers, in wheelchairs … people in pain and in despair.

If my prayer petitions were not granted, I would still be okay in the following months and years to come. If these people's prayer petitions were not granted, they may not make it the next day or the following week or month. Even if I know God is omnipotent, I felt undeserving and was humbled that my concerns were too trivial, so I prayed that their petitions be prioritized and be heard instead.

Since then, every time I pray, I have remembered the reality that somewhere out there, there are people struggling to survive one day at a time, thus, my personal petitions end up in the "by the way" portion of my prayer priorities.

But just to clarify it, this has nothing to do why my prayer for my Plus One remains unanswered. It remains unanswered because it's my fault. God has been sending prospects my way but clearly, I wasn't doing my part.

Plus One Plus None

9 NO FILTER

After I stopped praying version 16, I reflected -

Do I really want to have a boyfriend and get married? Or am I just half-hearted about it? Because if I badly and seriously want to get married, how come I cannot get a simple task of getting a person's name right? Am I still not ready after all these years?

Okay, that last question actually made me cringe.

Since the time I did the math, opened up myself to blind dates, tried online dating and edited my prayer from version 8 to version 16, guess how many years have passed?

5 years!!!

How can time fly so fast?! And why does it seem to go by faster as you get older???

Yes, 5 years have quickly gone by which makes me - *drum roll* - 42 today!!! Yikes, right?!

Here I am – already forty-plus and still half-hearted and uncertain about wanting marriage.

I reflected and realized some important things:

1. Though I removed all filters in Prayer v16, deep in my heart, I still hoped that my Plus One would have the traits I listed down in my Prayer v8 because the older I got

and the more I came to know myself better, I noticed the pickier I became. Pickier not in the discriminating sense but there's better clarity on what I want and don't want, and what I can tolerate and cannot tolerate.

To be clear, I am not looking for chemistry or fireworks. I also don't believe in the concept of having just one soulmate. What I am looking for are an intellectual connection, common values and shared sense of humor. This explains why I easily lose interest in a date when I detect something that is off.

Also, if you've ever been in a past relationship, you well know that some things you find adorable in your partner during the early stage of your relationship would no longer be as adorable after some time. The very same things could be a source of annoyance and drive you nuts. I have not only experienced this, but I have also seen this happen to other couples - couples so madly in love with each other when they got married, then later on transformed into two total strangers who cannot stand having even a simple conversation with each other.

Within this context, my simple logic is - if there's something about a person which bothers or annoys me now, what makes me think that it would be less annoying moving forward? Imagine, this someone would be the person I would be spending a lot of time with for the rest of my life. He is the first person I would see when I wake up in the morning and the last person I would see when I close my eyes at night. If today he has certain habits or traits that bother or annoy me like being too trivial, illogical, indecisive or he has strong negative opinions on topics which are very important to me, or we have some misalignment in values like how he treats people, I could already predict what's bound to happen between the two of us in the years to come.

Perhaps people could change and that may be true for some, but for most people, change is difficult especially as one gets older. Also, the motivation of a person when he decides to change is equally important. A person should change because he is doing it for himself and not to please someone else, otherwise, there may be a tendency to backslide when he no longer wishes to please the other person.

There's a popular saying taken from a poem by Alfred Lord Tennyson that goes, "*It is better to have loved and lost than never to have loved at all,*" but for a logical person like me, it is better to forego love if there are clear signs at the onset that it is more likely to be a loss.

2. When I get home after a long day's work, I am physically and mentally exhausted. I don't have the energy to prepare food that's why most of the time, I just eat out or have a vegetable and fruit smoothie. It's the quickest meal to prepare - 15 minutes tops from preparation to washing the dishes.

Given this reality, I wonder - how can I even care for another person when I don't have the energy and cannot even do it well for myself now?

That's why I admire all hands-on parents able to do gazillions of things for their spouses and kids considering that they are busier and more exhausted than me. I hope they realize that what they are doing is not just amazing but it's an extraordinary feat.

3. I've always feared pregnancy and childbirth since the first time I saw a childbirth video in school while we were taking up the Reproductive System during my puberty years. The image of a baby slathered with blood coming out of a woman in excruciating pain petrified me.

The thought of a baby living inside my body and moving inside my tummy terrifies me. I am careless and clumsy. What if the baby gets hurt because of my carelessness? What if I eat something that affects the development of the baby?

My back aches just carrying my laptop to and from the office. What more if I am carrying a baby inside my body for 9 months, 24/7?

When I sleep, I toss and turn a lot. What if the baby gets hurt while I unconsciously toss and turn at night?

I haven't even started with my fears about childbirth - the long labor, pain, blood, stitches... I once had an operation on my right shoulder that required stitches for a 1.5-inch long wound. I did not look the entire time the doctor performed the procedure. And after the operation, I quivered every time I had to clean the wound.

I am also super scared of blood. There have been years when I skipped my annual medical check-ups because of my fear of blood extraction. I can't even look at movie or tv show scenes where there is blood. And just listening to stories about accidents or medical-related situations where there is mention of blood makes me weak and dizzy.

And on taking care of a baby - I am scared to carry infants. I don't carry babies until they are a few months' old and I am certain they could hold up their heads firmly. Am I even capable of bathing a baby? How do you even bathe one if you cannot carry one? I'm an ignorant coward I know.

Though some say having a baby would trigger your mother's instincts so there's nothing to worry about because you would naturally know what to do, but I've also heard from a few moms that their mother's instincts did not kick in - at least for bathing their babies. They had to ask their own moms or get help to bathe their babies in the early weeks and months.

Then there's breastfeeding and milk pumping... and raising and disciplining kids. Do I even have the energy and patience to do those?

There's also the emotional aspect - when your child is hurt or sick, you feel for the child. What if he/she undergoes a difficult period in his/her life? As it is now, I get emotional when I hear sad news about other kids - kids who are sick, who get bullied, who are neglected, who have disabilities, who commit suicide, who are abused, who get victimized, etc. I don't even personally know these kids, but they are in my thoughts and prayers at night for several days and weeks after I hear about their heartbreaking stories. And every time I think about the possibility if I were the mom of any of these kids, I always arrive at the same conclusion - that I would definitely break and have a melt-down.

I could be stoic about bad things that happen to me because I am in full control of my thoughts and feelings, but when bad things happen to others especially to my loved ones, it's very difficult for me because I can only do so much. I can listen, help and support them but how they ultimately process their thoughts and emotions is entirely up to them.

But don't get me wrong, I adore babies and kids. I super love my nieces and nephews. My heart melts at the sight of babies. Kids bring me so much joy that there was even a point when it crossed my mind to become a pre-school teacher that I dropped my MBA to shift to an early childhood education program (but that's another story altogether). But what I fear is everything about pregnancy, motherhood, parenthood and everything between.

Bringing a child into the world is the greatest miracle of life. I have the highest regard for all parents out there who have dedicated their lives in raising and taking care of their children. I think there is no amount of professional achievement or wealth accumulation that could ever beat a parent's accomplishment in loving and raising their kids well.

4. I love my life and I am happy and contented where I am. I could do whatever I want to do in my life with very few considerations even for major decisions. Here are some of them:

- I can travel whenever I want and without having to worry about leaving my place unattended for weeks or months.

- I can quit my job if I want to and even take a pay cut if I really like something else better.

- I can forget myself when exploring a place without having to report my whereabouts to anyone for a full uninterrupted day, or even days.

- I have manageable expenses which I can easily cut down if I need to.

- I can spend time with my nieces and nephews based on my availability and easily return them to their parents when I already need to do other things.

- I can pursue further studies if I want to.

- I can plan my personal activities at my own schedule and pace.

- I can eat whatever food I want when I'm home or eat out whenever I feel like going out.

- I can rest, sleep and do nothing the whole day on weekends if want to.

In short, my life is simple, and I have no complex problems.

Am I being too selfish that I don't want to give up what I have?

I know some of the concerns I listed above are actually solvable if I really want to get married such as —

Have no time or too tired to cook? There's food delivery.

Need to have alone time regularly? Have individual bedrooms for alone time and a common master bedroom for couple's time.

Too tired at the end of a workday? Change jobs.

Scared to give birth? Adopt a baby.

Don't know how to carry a baby or bathe a baby? Hire help - at least in the first few weeks or months.

Clearly, the problem is all me. I don't want to risk my existing happy and comfortable life with something that is not guaranteed to be equally happy and comfortable even if there's a chance that something could be even happier and more comfortable. Yes, I know I am such a selfish wimp. So, to those who secretly wonder if there is something odd about me that's why I am still single, yes, they are correct.

I am picky even if I have a lot of imperfections and annoying traits myself.

I have given up conceptually even before actually trying or exploring possible solutions.

I want everything to be scoped out even if I know a lot of things in life are unpredictable and unknown, and sometimes, the only way to know if you can handle the unpredictable and unknown is for you to just dive into it and deal with it as life unfolds.

Clearly, I want high probabilities of success and minimal risks. I must keep in mind though that like any investment, whether financial or non-financial, that –

high risk = high returns
low risk = low returns
no risk = status quo.

10 INCESSANT INTERROGATION

For as long as I have no boyfriend, or stay unmarried or I am childless, for sure I would either be a conversational piece or subject in scrutiny.

Just the other weekend, I was with my mom and she bumped into an acquaintance while we were strolling in the mall. Here's how their conversation went while the three of us walked together towards the supermarket –

Acquaintance: *Is she your daughter or granddaughter?*
(Sorry, I had to include this because this is the only positive thing from the conversation. *Lol.*)
My Mom: *Daughter*
Acquaintance: *So, is she married with kids?*
My Mom: *She's still single.*
Acquaintance: *What?! How old is she?*
My Mom: *Forty-something.*
Acquaintance: *Forty-something and she's still unmarried?! What is she waiting for?!* <Short pause> *Although a lot of women in their forties are still able to give birth these days so I think she could still make a baby before her eggs expire.*

It was the usual conversation between two moms like

how moms would talk about their kids in front of their kids when their kids were in kindergarten, except the subject of this conversation was a 42-year old daughter.

The more difficult conversations though are when you are being directly interrogated. I noticed though how I answered intrusive questions or reacted to comments have drastically changed over the years - from fascination to wonder, from annoyance to exhaustion, from evasion to comic relief.

In my younger years (in my 20s), I tried to give serious answers because it was the first time I got asked these questions and there was the linear storyline to follow.

Scenario 1
Interrogator: *When are you getting married?*
Me: *Maybe between age xx and xx.*

Scenario 2
Interrogator: *When are you getting married?*
Me: *Maybe after I accomplish xx milestone.*

Then after some time (in my early-30s), I realized that by answering the questions, I was allowing others to pressure me. The problem was - I was still nowhere near marrying! So, I started evading the questions.

Scenario 1
Interrogator: *When are you getting married?*
Me: *How are the kids??*

Scenario 2
Interrogator: *When are you getting married?*
Me: *Wait, have you heard about XX news??*

Scenario 3
Interrogator: *When are you getting married?*
Me: *How was your trip?! Tell me about it first.*

This could be really effective if you can successfully pick a topic that is more interesting to the interrogator. And don't forget - always end with a question. Then, after every answer, just continue to have follow-up questions until time runs out and it's time to say goodbye.

Later on, I got comfortable with my single status (in my mid-30s). Not sure if this is a natural phase of acceptance as part of aging but anyway, I started answering the questions again but I gave really silly answers.

Scenario 1
Interrogator 1: *When are you getting married?*
Me: *May*
Interrogator: *Wow, congratulations! When in May?*
Me: *May it come true.*

Scenario 2
Interrogator: *When are you getting married?*
Me: *As soon as you'll introduce me to my groom.*

Scenario 3
Interrogator: *When are you getting married?*
Me: *Are you going to give me a date if I'm not getting married yet?*

Scenario 4
Interrogator: *When are you getting married?*
Me: *December 8 but no year yet. My wedding venue reservation is on auto-renewal every year.*

Scenario 5
Interrogator: *When are you getting married?*
Me: *When you stop complaining about married life.*

But then one day, I realized - why do I have to answer the interrogation when most of the people who ask me are not even close to me nor do they have any bearing in my life? The topic just happens to be their choice of small talk and conversation filler. And so, from that day on (in my late-30s), I regarded the questions as rhetorical questions.

> Interrogator: *When are you getting married?*
> Me: *Hahaha....*
> Interrogator: *Don't you want to get married?*
> Me: *Hahaha...*
> Interrogator: *Seriously, do you want to get married or not?*
> Me: *Hahaha...*

Usually, after the second or third question, the interrogator either changes the topic or walks out on me. It consistently works all the time.

As for the "*Are you single or married?*" question, I recently tried a bolder way to answer the question and it went like this –

> Interrogator: *Are you single or married?*
> Me: *I'm a spinster.*
> Interrogator (with shocked face): *Oh...*

The interrogator never asked my age and she changed the topic instead.

Another time, someone asked me, "*How old are you?*" first and here's how it went –

> Interrogator: *How old are you?*
> Me: *I'm already old because I'm an old maid.*
> Interrogator (with stunned face): *Oh ...*
> End of conversation.

I think it catches people off-guard when you proudly declare yourself a spinster or an old maid. But the most important thing to be able to pull off these conversations is you must be comfortable with yourself. I naturally laugh a lot, I'm very straightforward and I am very secure with my single status that's why I could easily pull these off. But if you have a different personality or if you're not that comfortable with your single status, then some other creative approach may work for you. Just continue to experiment until you find what comfortably works for you.

Also remember - the lesser info and the shorter your answers are (or the more irrelevant your answers are), the more likely the topic would be averted.

As much as possible, do not attempt to answer the questions too seriously unless you are with your closest friends or circle of trust. Attempting to answer them seriously when with acquaintances or strangers may sometimes lead to a debate where each party would try to convince each other that being married or being single is better than the other status, but neither is better. Either could be good or bad depending on how a person makes out of her life and that is always relative to oneself.

*****

11 INDISPUTABLY COMFORTABLE

Some good news - among relatives and friends, I noticed that the cross-examination has become less frequent. I think they may have accepted my status as a spinster, or they may have given up on me after I have kept adjusting my target age of getting married.

When I was in my early 20s, I said it was 30.
When I turned 30, I said it was 35.
When I turned 35, I said it was 40.

Now, I am past 40 already and I don't even have a prospective boyfriend, so my last official statement was that my target age of getting married is when I become a golden girl - 50!

I still get a handful of unsolicited advice and comments such as -

It's okay if you're still single. Single life is so much simpler.
Singles have fewer problems and fewer expenses. Good for you.
I wish I were still single...
You're on the right track - don't settle for less.

To be fair, some really mean it especially those who have experienced or are experiencing relationship problems or those who know of other single people who live equally fulfilling lives. But there are also some people who say these things to provide words of comfort.

But the thing is - they don't have to tell me these things because I should know better as I have been living the single life for two decades. And they need not give me words of comfort either because single life is very, very comfortable which is precisely one reason why it is so hard to give it up.

If your biggest reason for staying single is because you don't want to give up the freedom and comfort, guess what? Even Charles Darwin thought so too at one point in his life.

Yes, Charles Darwin had musings on whether to marry or not to marry. In 1838, around age 29, he wrote about the pros and cons of marrying and not marrying in his journal. You have to look for the complete version of Darwin's journal entries online to get the full context as this is only an overview and my interpretation may be incomplete and inaccurate.

But in gist, under "*If not marry*", Darwin wrote down the various places he could visit. He also listed down some potential activities he could do if he was not traveling. Then under "*If marry*", he wrote "*means limited*", "*feel duty to work for money*" and a whole slew of other things such as what profession he may do if he is a married man.

Then a few months later, Darwin revisited the subject. This time, he factored in the value of having a lifetime partner. Under "*Marry*", he listed down details such as having children and having a "*constant companion and friend in old age*". Then at the end of the list, he wrote that such things were "*good for one's health*" but were "*terrible loss of time*". But he also added that it was "*intolerable to think of spending one's whole life, like a neuter bee, working, working and nothing after all*".

Then under "*Not Marry*", Darwin wrote things like "*no children*" and "*no one to care for in old age*". He also wrote things like having "*freedom to go where one liked*", "*conversation of clever men at clubs*", "*not forced to visit relatives, & to bend in every trifle*", among many others. At the end of the list, he wrote that if you have many children, you are "*forced to gain one's bread*". "But then, he wrote, "*it is very bad for one's health to work too much*".

Guess what was Darwin's conclusion after listing down all the pros and cons? To marry!

Then he went through another list of pros and cons. This time it was for *Marrying Soon* versus *Marrying Late*. But I won't expound on that anymore. Marrying Soon is no longer an option for me. The musings more applicable now are "*Marrying Late*" versus "*Marrying Later*". *Lol.*

Anyway, going back to Darwin, six months after he wrote his ruminations on *Marrying Soon* versus *Marrying Late*, Darwin got married to a woman named Emma. He and Emma had 10 children, and they remained together until Darwin's death in 1882. *Awww…*

Again, you must check out Darwin's original journal entries for the complete context and for better appreciation. You might uncover nuggets of wisdom and insights from him. Even if it meant giving up freedom and comfort, Darwin still decided to marry.

12 REFLECTIONS ON TWILIGHT

Am I not afraid to grow old alone? I used to be super worried and scared of it but not anymore. How did I conquer my fear?

I occasionally visit a home for the aged to do volunteer work. I have a soft spot for the elderly because they remind me of my grandparents, parents, godparents, and uncles and aunts who have imparted wisdom in me which I have never quite understood until I became an adult. Also, I once learned from a social worker that more people visit and volunteer in institutions for kids than for the elderly, so I noted where help is more needed.

Anyway, even at the home for the aged, there was no escaping my status and age. The grandaunts and granduncles asked the usual age and civil status questions. Some are suffering from various stages of Alzheimer's disease so it's no surprise too if you get asked the same questions every 15 minutes.

Anyway, one time, two grandaunts asked me -
Are you married? Do you have kids?
I replied-
Oh, I'm not married yet. And I don't have kids.
Grandaunt #1 excitedly exclaimed -

Oh, we're the same! She isn't also married! The two of us are both old maids. <as she points to herself and grandaunt #2>

Grandaunt #2 looked at me and said -

It's okay even if you're not married. You see those 3? <she points to 3 other grandaunts in wheelchairs> *They are all married and with kids but look at them, they still ended up here like us.*

Obviously, they wanted to reassure me it was okay to stay unmarried by making a point that whether you marry or not, the final destination could be potentially the same. Remember, this was also the same point which my mom told me when my uncle was pushing me to get married so I would have kids who could take care of me when I grow old.

But nope, this is not the reason I am no longer afraid to grow old alone. Yes, it was a good point raised by grandaunts and granduncles while we are at the topic of growing old but the reason I am no longer afraid to grow old alone was actually so glaring but I was just oblivious of it the entire time. And the reason is that I have been all alone for the longest time and I am super okay with it. In fact, I look forward to being alone at the end of each day, remember?

Have I told you that my place was designed for only one person because I don't like to entertain guests? I only have a small round table and one chair in the dining area.

For my dinnerware, I have only 2 sets of plates, cups, and saucers. Two sets not because the second one is for a guest, but two because the other one is my spare set for the next meal, in case I was too lazy to wash the dishes in the earlier meal.

In my living room, there is no sofa. I have only a rocker recliner that could sit one person, and also a work desk and one office chair.

In my bedroom, it's just my bed and closet.

That's it. That's everything I have at home. Thus, in

the rare times when some friends had to drop by my place to get something, it's always SRO unless they don't mind squatting on the floor.

You might be wondering if I don't get bored or lonely when I am home alone. For whatever reason, I never run out of things to do at home. I could read or write for hours and be oblivious to everything else. And even if I am just lying in my bed looking at the ceiling or staring at a blank wall, I never get bored too as I could daydream for hours. Yes, I have well-developed imagination skills which I think was a result of not having a lot of toys when I was a kid.

So psychologically and emotionally, I have the DNA to joyfully grow old alone. The only thing I need to work on is on the financial front. I must make sure that I set aside enough money for retirement so I can afford a caregiver and a comfortable life when I am old and unable to take care of myself. Though I also don't mind staying in a home for the aged. I'm very much at home when I visit elderly homes.

My reflection did not just stop at growing old alone. It went all the way to my passing away. Consistent with my introvert nature, I want to exit the world quietly. I know of people who worry about their future wakes and their greatest fear is - what if very few people (or none at all outside of the family) would show up at their wakes? In my case, I don't even want my relatives and friends to know once I have passed away. I also don't want to have a wake and let them see me dead. I'd rather have them remember me the last time they saw me alive. For me, what truly matters in the end are the moments loved ones have spent with me and the words they have told me when I was still alive.

I also don't want a tomb. Why? Because the space which my tomb would occupy would be of better use for someone who wants to be remembered. At the end of my life, I just want to blend in with Mother Nature and do my part in fertilizing the soil and be forgotten.

But did you know that for one's dead body to be useful to the soil, the body should not be embalmed (as that delays the body's rate of decay), nor should it be encased in a metal or non-biodegradable casket, nor be cremated since cremated ash is too sterile and does not supply nutrients back to the earth? I have yet to figure out the best way to become fertilizer. ;-)

13 IF YOU BADLY WANT IT, YOU'LL DO IT

If you are nearing forty or are forty-plus already, don't fret. Forty is the new thirty just as when we told ourselves that thirty is the new twenty when we turned 30. And when we reach 50, for sure, we are going to tell ourselves that fifty is the new forty. *Lol.*

Anyway, at forty, there are so many things you could still do! And while you're still single, do not stop pursuing your personal goals and learning new things. Guess what I crossed off from my DWIC List recently? I learned how to swim and overcame my fear of water! Yes, I only learned how to swim in my forties.

I enrolled in a late evening swim class. Why late evening? So that it's dark and I won't be embarrassed and be self-conscious about flapping and kicking aimlessly in the water.

During the first session, while waiting for our swim coach, here was my conversation with my two classmates.

I asked -
Why did you sign up for the class?
Classmate #1 replied -

Oh, I want to be more efficient with my strokes, so I won't easily get tired during triathlons.

Gulp. He is a triathlete! Are you kidding me?!

Classmate #2 replied -

I want to improve my form. And just like him (pointing to Classmate #1), *I want my strokes to be more efficient, so I won't tire easily.*

Both of my classmates know how to swim! Am I in the right class?!

Classmate #2 then turned to me and asked –

How about you? Why did you sign up for this swim class?

I answered -

For basic survival...

Anyway, I was so determined to learn how to swim I spent hours practicing swimming drills on my own between classes, and I watched a lot of swimming videos. In two weeks, my coach asked me to swim across a 25-meter pool, 8-feet deep at its deepest. He asked me to swim starting from the deepest part so that if I don't make it across the full 25 meters, I would hopefully make it to the shallow part.

But when I went to the 8-feet deep portion of the pool, oh my, I got so scared that I was holding on to the pool's ladder for like 10 minutes and I was negotiating with my coach if we can just postpone my first attempt to the next session. Even if I knew my coach was there, and there was a lifeguard on standby, the thought of 8-feet deep paralyzed me.

My coach held his ground. He said this same thing would happen again in the next session so I might as well do it now. Another coach suggested that I should try standing at the bottom of the pool to get a feel on how deep it really is. I followed this advice but while still holding on to the pool's ladder.

I sank myself and stood at the bottom of the pool. I did this twice and it greatly helped because I realized that when you reach the bottom of the pool, you get pushed up to the surface. So, I thought even if I fail and sink, I would still get pushed up to the surface, and maybe when I reach the surface, I could hold on to the ledge for safety. And guess what? I successfully made it across the full 25 meters on my first attempt. Yay!

In 2 months, I tried swimming in an Olympic-size pool and also successfully made it across the full 50 meters on my first attempt (and all my succeeding attempts). It was just amazing!

What is the key takeaway from this? This is proof that when you badly want something, you will find ways and make time to do it, even if that something seems impossible, scary and embarrassing.

As you've seen, I was able to commit and spend a lot of time in overcoming my fear of water but not (yet) in overcoming my discomfort in meeting more EPs. Thus, if you prioritize a lot of other things which leaves you no time to meet new people (or to date), ask yourself - are you really sure you want to have a boyfriend and eventually get married? Because your actions could be saying otherwise.

But then again, the good news is, you could always find activities where there are also opportunities to meet new people so it's like hitting two birds with one stone. Unfortunately, in my case, the activity I chose - swimming - is a solitary activity like most of my other activities.

*****

By the way, it's very important that you keep yourself fit. It does not only make you feel good but also makes you look good, or even make you look younger than your age. But did you know that looking younger than your age could be complicated too?

Case in point - there was this guy who struck a conversation with me a couple of months back while I was swimming and he asked for my number. I knew right away that he is younger than me because he doesn't look like the typical men from my age group – at least based on his hairline. But what can I possibly tell him? That he shouldn't get my number because we're from different generations?

Since I didn't know what to say and he seemed courteous, I just gave my number. Maybe he just wants to be friends.

Anyway, the guy started sending me friendly messages, which was fine. Then he asked me out for coffee which was still fine since we could be friends. Occasionally, he would join me for swimming and evening walks. Then almost every day, he sent me messages, photos and short video clips of what he found interesting during the day like food, the sunset, colorful fishes he saw while scuba diving...

Uh-oh.

And because of the age thing, I did not want us to become more than friends. I had to figure out how to tell him. I was torn between telling him face-to-face versus mobile chat. But then I thought, if I would do it face-to-face, it would be very awkward when I reveal my age as it won't be easy to stifle a jaw-dropping reaction. So, I waited for the right opportunity to bring it up casually over mobile chat.

Finally, one day, an opportunity came to segue the age discussion. We were chatting about a project I was undertaking and to encourage me, he messaged –

I am sure you can do that because you're smart.

I typed back -

I am sure I can do it not because I am smart, but because I have wisdom since I am already old. That's why always remember I am just your big sister, okay?

Long pause. He was not in typing mode either. I guess he was super shocked!

Then after a while, I saw from the chat app window he started typing and this was his reply –

Really? I thought we were of the same age. If it's not inappropriate to ask, may I know how old are you?

I didn't want to reveal my age to him! So, I typed back -

Please don't ask me that. It's so embarrassing to reveal my age! Just be the one to share your age and maybe I can introduce you to my younger friends.

Guess how old is he? Thirty-one years old! We are eleven years apart. And he thought we were of the same age?! He definitely needs to see an ophthalmologist.

14 TAKING FULL ACCOUNTABILITY

In my two decades of being single, I have heard of countless reasons and explanations for one's single or unmarried status such as –

Everyone I meet is either married, has a boyfriend, or likes guys too.
Guys never approach me.
Guys never ask me out.
I haven't met the right person yet.
No one is setting me up for dates.
I'm so unlucky in love.
I'm too busy at work.
I don't have time to meet new people.
I am so tired of dating.
I am so tired of failed relationships.
I am so tired of trying.
I am so tired of waiting.
Maybe it's not the right time for me yet.
If it comes, it comes.
Not everyone is cut out for married life and maybe I am one of them.

Yada, yada, yada.

Have you noticed that the reasons given are rarely within one's control? They are often caused by someone else or some other thing but never by the person herself.

But really whatever one's status is - whether she has a Plus One or a Plus None - is ultimately the person's choice. One's status is an outcome of one's aggregate actions and decisions made in the past.

As you've noticed throughout my story, I always held myself accountable. Initially though, that wasn't the case. Like most single women, I used to blurt out the usual excuses such as *"It's so hard to find dates"* or *"I don't have time to date"* until it occurred to me – how come there are women out there who are equally busy (or even busier) yet they are able to get dates and find time to date? Clearly, I must be doing something wrong.

I used the "The 5 Whys" technique to reflect more deeply. If you're not familiar with "The 5 Whys", it's a simple but powerful technique to find the root cause of any problem by asking yourself *why* five times -

Why am I not able to find dates? Because I don't get to meet a lot of people.

Why don't I get to meet a lot of people? Because I am busy at work and don't have time to go out after work.

Why don't I have time to go out after work? Because I go home after work to rest and do other things.

Why do I go home after work and have time to do other things but not have the time to go out to meet people? Because I prefer to be at home alone.

I didn't even reach the fifth why to make me realize everything was my fault.

So, single and unmarried people are not single and unmarried because they did not have a choice. It is their choice to be single and to stay unmarried - whether the decision was made consciously or unconsciously.

Yes, if you're still single and unmarried, it's the outcome of all your past actions and decisions.

If you say you don't get to meet a lot of eligible prospects, then it could mean you have decided not to make time to meet new people or not to try other forms of dating. Because if you really want to have more EPs, there is a big population of prospects out there, not just within your geographic location, but globally.

If you say guys never approach you or do not ask you out, it could mean you have decided to maintain whatever demeanor you have instead of trying to be more approachable, friendly and responsive.

If you say you haven't met the right person yet, it could mean you have decided not to put yourself out there, or had you put yourself out there, it could mean you have decided to never settle for anyone lesser than your ideal person.

If you say you are unlucky in love, then it could mean you have already claimed that your fate in love, no matter what you do, shall be unfavorable and miserable.

If you say you are tired of dating, tired of failed relationships, tired of trying, or tired of waiting, then it could mean you have made the decision you have reached your threshold and that's it for you. You have given up.

If you say you don't have the time to date and meet people, then it could mean you have made the decision that other things in your life are more important than finding a potential partner.

If you say you are not ready yet, then it could mean you are still unprepared emotionally or financially, or you still have unresolved fears, or you are not willing to take risks.

If you say you're not cut out for married life, then it could mean you have made the decision that you don't want to change yourself and your life to prepare for a different role.

But look, there is no right or wrong in any of these decisions. Each one of us has a different set of circumstances so whatever decision you make is relative to yourself. The point is - staying or ending up being single or unmarried is ultimately your personal choice based on your aggregate decisions and actions.

But even if you have decided to remain single in your life, it does not mean you must stick to an unmarried status forever. Anytime you realize that you want to have someone in your life, just go for it! Make it happen.

And even if you enjoy your single status (like I do), please do not close the door on opportunities. Remain open to new friendships and dating opportunities. Like in my case - if someone sets me up or someone interesting asks me out for a date, I still say yes. Besides, I need to make new friends today if I want to change the trajectory of my life and steer it away from becoming a total recluse.

15 HAPPY ENDING

Have you heard about the story of a fisherman and an enterprising tourist written by a German writer named Heinrich Böll? There are many versions of the story circulating online but the story goes like this (based on Böll's core plot combined with some dialogues from enhanced versions):

There was a businessman who went on a vacation in a small coastal village on the west coast of Europe.

One morning as the businessman tourist was taking photographs, he noticed a shabbily dressed local fisherman who was taking a nap in his fishing boat. Disappointed with the lazy attitude of the fisherman since he already stopped fishing and was already napping considering it was still very early in the day, he approached the fisherman.

"How long did it take you to catch those fishes?" asked the businessman.

"Only a little while, señor," the fisherman replied.

"Why don't you catch more fishes?" the businessman asked.

"I already have enough for my family and to give away to friends, señor," the fisherman replied.

"But what do you do with the rest of your time?" the

businessman asked.

"I sleep late, fish a little, play with my children, take a siesta with my wife, and stroll the village each evening, where I sip wine and play guitar with my amigos. I have a full and busy life, señor," the fisherman answered.

The businessman laughed and told the fisherman —

"I have an MBA degree and I can help you. You should spend more time fishing, and with the proceeds, you can buy a bigger boat. In no time, you can buy more boats until you have a fleet."

"Then what, señor?" the fisherman asked.

"Then one day, you could build a small cold storage plant, and later on a pickling factory. Then you can build a fish restaurant, and later on export directly to places around the world without a middleman," the businessman explained.

"But señor, how long will this take?" the fisherman asked.

"15 to 20 years," the businessman answered.

"But what then, señor?" the fisherman asked.

The businessman laughed again and replied —

"When the time is right, your company can go public to raise capital for further expansion, and you'll become very rich. You will make millions!"

"Millions, señor? Then what?" the fisherman asked.

The businessman replied —

"Then you could retire and move to a small coastal village, where you would sleep late, fish a little, play with your kids, take a siesta with your wife, and stroll the village in the evenings where you could sip wine and play guitar with your amigos."

The enlightened businessman walked away pensively with no trace of pity for the fisherman, only a little envy.

*****

The reason I like this fisherman story and why it struck a chord in me is because some people are so busy chasing certain society-expected status without taking time to reflect if that is really the life they want to live.

To the naked eye, some people are living lives that may

look plain and ordinary, but they are actually the ones living the ultimate dream life. They may not have the trappings of success but they enjoy real freedom as they do not have to do things for the sake of pleasing others or upholding their positions, nor are they enslaved to keep on acquiring material possessions and living certain lifestyles to preserve their status and image.

The fisherman's life is the dream life - but not in the sense that the fisherman is married with kids. Actually, in the original story, there was no mention of "*play with your kids, take a siesta with your wife, play guitar with your amigos...*" so the fisherman could have been unmarried. The exact words of the businessman about the dream life in the original story were –

Then without a care in the world, you could sit here in the harbor, doze in the sun, and look at the glorious sea.

See, the fisherman could have possibly been single. But no, the civil status of the fisherman is not the point here. Regardless of his status, the important lesson is - you must know what really matters in your life so you don't chase unnecessary things only to realize that the life you are already living is exactly the life you've always dreamt of living.

Like in my case – I started with a vision that I would be married with kids because it's the only path I knew as a kid. And though I have been side-tracked many times, I stuck to this vision because all the probing questions I was bombarded with in my 20s and 30s all lead to this vision. There was no other path.

It was only when I started questioning myself at different stages in my life why I kept doing actions which are counter-productive to this vision when I slowly began to realize that it clearly doesn't look like I want the vision to happen. Though I claimed I wanted to find a boyfriend and get married, I still preferred to stay home most of the time, gave up online dating too soon, refused to go out on second and third dates when the guy wasn't my type and I was not willing to give up a lot of comforts in life, among many other things. And even after acknowledging the priceless joys of being married (being able to perform the greatest miracle in life by giving birth and having the chance to perform the best role in life which is to love and raise kids), I still preferred to stay in my guaranteed happy place instead of taking a chance at something, though not guaranteed, could be even way happier and more rewarding.

But I also know that there may be a possibility in the future that things may change and I may not feel the same way as I feel now. Life happens. Circumstances change. We evolve. If one day I suddenly realize I want to be with someone, then I'll just go for it. I'll proactively do what I need to do to increase my chances of finding a Plus One. I know it won't be easy because I would be older by then but I have to live with it because it is one of the possible consequences of the choice I made in my life today. What's important is I am making this choice today with eyes wide open and with full acceptance of all the possible trade-offs.

This may not be the happy ending that you want to hear but this is real life unfiltered. But I'll give you a happier ending - the ending that matters most is not that of my story but that of your story - where you want to direct your life's trajectory based on how you want your life story to turn out to be.

If by chance, you somehow saw yourself in me but you didn't like the way how my life turned out to be or where it is headed, you know what to do - just do the exact opposite of everything I did! *Lol.*

Be bolder, be more open, take more risks, and be crazier than me. If your life revolves around your home and workplace and you have very limited opportunities to meet new people, you could already predict how your life would look like in 5 years, 10 years, 15 years ...

If you seriously want to get married, you have to do

something different today to alter your life's trajectory. Coasting along your current trajectory of *work - home -same friends - work - home- same friends* routine won't bring you closer to meeting your Plus One but it would bring you closest to having a Plus None.

Remember too that the older you get, the scarcer EPs become. And EPs within your age range would most likely prefer younger women. My mid-30s blind date preferred "more mature" women whom he defined as 25 to 28 years old, remember?

It's a harsh reality but men in their 40s would most likely prefer women in their 30s, men in their 50s would most likely prefer women in their 40s or even younger. As we get older, our preferred age range doesn't intersect with most men's preferred age range, and this discrepancy may even get wider as we get older.

So, if you are single and you whole-heartedly know that you want to get married and have kids, by all means, do something about your situation now. If you still slack around and do nothing, at least recognize that you are doing what you are doing (or rather not doing) in your life with your eyes wide open.

Finally, I want to leave you with the 10 most important lessons from my single life.

1. Write your Do-While-I-Can List (DWIC List) and pursue the things on your list while you can, because remember, we have different life spans, energy levels and physical conditions. Some of us may complete a lifetime without reaching old age, and some of us may no longer be physically able to do certain activities even before reaching our prime years.

Your DWIC List won't just empower you to get to know yourself better but also enable you to grow and do things you love, and do them on your own without depending on someone. It's part of the process of completing yourself so you don't have to rely on someone to make you feel complete.

Just make sure that your DWIC List is not all about leisure goals. Also include new skills you want to learn, improvements you need to make, financial and career milestones you want to achieve, healthy habits you want to develop, advocacies and volunteer work you want to pursue, and spiritual activities you want to practice more regularly.

2. Whatever your situation in life is (not just your civil status but in financial, career, health and fitness, etc.), that is the aggregate outcome of the various little decisions you have made in your life. You are fully accountable for your life.

How your life has turned out so far and how it is turning out to be, that is on you. There is nothing or no one else to blame. In as much as there are a lot of external factors in your life, the primary driver of your life is no one else but you.

It is always easier to blame external circumstances such as it is the fault of other people, or of an unexpected event, or a misfortune, however, that is short of saying you could not do anything to improve your situation. The thing is, you always have the power to do something.

Saying there is lack of opportunities is not a valid reason. Perhaps the reason for your lack of opportunities is because self-imposed restrictions narrowed down your options. If for example, you complain there are not a lot of dating opportunities, maybe (like me) you don't go out enough to socialize. If you badly want dates but no one is asking you out, there are other solutions - you can ask friends to set you up for dates or you can try online dating where there are thousands of prospects out there all over the world whom you can chat with and get to know better.

Or, if for example, you complain there are not a lot of job opportunities out there, maybe you are only open to specific job types of a certain pay grade in specific industries within a particular geographic location. Because if you badly want to earn a living, there are a lot of opportunities globally including output-based online projects which do not discriminate on age, gender or location. You have the power to create more opportunities for yourself if only you allow yourself to be more open.

But let's just say that some things that have happened in your life could be attributable to external circumstances like natural calamities, accidents, and tragedies. You still have the power within you to bounce back if you want to. It's not easy but you can if you really, really want to.

For instance, once upon a time, we lost our house and all our possessions during a volcanic eruption. It was unthinkable for me how we could rise above such a tragedy both emotionally and financially. But instead of having a "*victim mentality*", I just focused on moving on and just finding humor in our circumstance.

It would have been easier for me to blame, complain and gripe about how life sucked but it's such a waste of energy that would not make the situation any better. And compared to what other people have gone through, our experience was nothing. Other people have suffered far more unimaginable and horrendous conditions in life and even lost loved ones but they have successfully made it through.

Yes, there may be variables in life which are unforeseen and which we cannot control, but there are some things we could still control. At the end of the day, we could control our thoughts, and we could control how we react and act on those unavoidable circumstances.

3. Never take time for granted. Days easily turn into weeks, weeks into months, months into years, and years into decades. Before you know it, you'll be 30, 35, 40, 45, 50...

Remember that time is the only wealth which we all have been given equally, and it is the only wealth which we need not work for to earn it. But unlike material wealth which you could still recover by working hard when you lose it, when it comes to time, once it has passed, you will never be able to recover it no matter what you do.

You are 25 years old only once. You are 30 years old only once. You are 35 years old only once. There's no stopping or rewinding time or our age.

How you spend your gift of time is what would ultimately define the trajectory of your life so please don't spend it mindlessly

If you recall when you were small kids, it seemed like the playing field was equal. Everyone had similar skill sets. Maybe some could solve math problems faster by a few seconds than others, but everyone was within close range in terms of life's trajectory.

After several years in school, the gaps in skills were more apparent such as who were good in academics, sports, leadership, social skills, performing arts, etc. But everyone's trajectories were generally still within a reasonable range.

But after a couple of decades, think about how huge the differences in the trajectories were. Some people who were chill, or quiet, or low-key, or unassuming did exceptionally well and are now doing meaningful work and advocacies. This means, along the way, they must have done something differently and have done it consistently that it changed the trajectory of their lives which is really very inspiring.

Emphasis on the words "different" and "consistent". One-time, big-time, radically different actions may alter the course of your trajectory but to keep your trajectory on the right path, it is the small actions which you do consistently over time that really matter.

4. If you really want something to happen in your life, you must make it happen. No amount of goal writing, brainstorming, planning, visualizing, claiming, praying, hoping, wishing, discussing, analyzing and waiting (even if you combine all these), can make it happen if you don't do

the real action.

To have a boyfriend, go out, make friends and date.

To lose weight, control your food intake and exercise.

If you are unhappy with your job, find a new job.

If you want to become financially independent, save and invest.

If you want to become a writer, write.

Intention should translate to real action. Even if you repeatedly announce your goals to everyone and claim they would happen someday, that someday would never arrive if you do not consistently do the basic action required to achieve your goal.

If you do not exert enough effort or you easily give up, it just means you do not want something badly. Because if you really want something badly, you would be willing to do uncomfortable and painful things and take risks to make it happen.

There is also no such thing as too busy or no time. Every time you say, *"I don't have time to do xx"*, it only means you have decided to do something else that you consider more important.

Do not leave your goals, dreams and wishes to pure hope, chance or luck. If you have life goals and dreams which you want to happen in your life by a certain age, make sure you have a clear plan and timeline in place.

What kind of plan? For example, if you envision yourself to be married with kids at age 35, then it means, you need to get pregnant at age 34. If you're pregnant at age 34, then it means you need to be married by age 33 or 34. If you're married at age 33, then it means you need to be engaged at age 32. If you're engaged at age 32, then it means you need to have a boyfriend by age 30 or 31. If you have a boyfriend at age 30 or 31, then it means you have to be actively dating at age 28 or 29. Of course, any of these stages could be longer or shorter (except for pregnancy, of course) or you can even skip some stages. But without a clear plan, you'll mostly likely end up with a moving target age and an indefinite timeline.

So, think about your target age and work backwards on how to achieve your goal so you can do the real action starting today to increase your chances of making it happen within your desired timeframe.

5. If you keep on doing the same thing, don't expect different results. Make some changes and improvements until you get the results you want, or until you realize something else is more important.

When you catch yourself feeling tired or frustrated because you think you have been giving it your best shot, but nothing is still happening, think again. Yes, it could be true that you have been spending a lot of time and exerting a lot of effort on something, but the question is - have you been doing the right action that yields the target outcome?

Making changes and improvements is not just about spending more time or exerting more effort on the same action. If the action does not yield the intended results, then the action is useless no matter how much time or effort you put into it. Thus, do not be too quick to complain that nothing seems to work no matter what you do. Instead of ranting and continuing what you are doing, reflect on what you have been doing ineffectively, and think of new ways on how to progress and move forward.

Just remember - if you do not do something differently today (and this isn't just about finding a boyfriend, or a husband, or starting your own family), you could already predict with some degree of accuracy how your life would turn out after 1 year, 3 years, 5 years, 10 years... It's definitely not going to be far from where you are right now. That is great if that is exactly how you pictured your life to be, but if that is not how you envisioned it to be, then it's time to do something differently now.

6. Live the life you want to live. Do not allow yourself to succumb to social pressure and live a life based on other people's expectations. Just because most people are xx

(e.g. married), you have to be xx (e.g. married) too.

You must set your own rules, standards and definition of success. Measure yourself based only on these rules, standards and definition of success. And when you measure and assess yourself, it should always be your current self against your past self (and not versus other people) because the only competition is against yourself.

If you see someone you think is doing exceptionally well, he/she should not be viewed as competition but as an inspiration. You could only be better than your old self and the other person could only be better than his/her old self. If you view life as a contest where one is better, smarter, more successful, or richer than the other, then you won't ever be totally free as you are subjecting yourself to the standards of others.

7. Uncomfortable conversations with intrusive people are inevitable so while stuck in one, you might as well get something out of it. Learn how to filter out advice and comments that do not make sense but graciously listen to those that make sense. These encounters are also great for character-building. If it is any consolation, some people do have sincerely good intentions.

Also, please remember that for many generations, women have been expected to marry and have kids by a certain age. Just imagine how unmarried women in earlier times were much more ostracized. For us who are unmarried today, we are actually living in kinder times though I hope there will come a time when we need not explain why we are unmarried. Maybe as the number of people who remain unmarried increases generation after generation, more people would realize that being single is as mainstream as being married.

8. Seriously commit to take care of yourself - eat properly, exercise regularly and dress neatly. It's hard for others to put you down emotionally during an interrogation if you feel good about yourself and if you look good.

Be inspired by countless married women with kids or single moms who have successfully maintained good fitness habits. If they were able to do it even after giving birth and while juggling multiple responsibilities, you can draw inspiration from them and use that as a motivation that you can do it too.

9. When you think about your life's regrets, do not be too quick to judge certain phases of your life as meaningless or generalize certain parts of your life as regrets.

Always remember that life is a collection of moments and a chain reaction of events, and if time were turned back and you would have done your life differently by omitting certain phases of your life and doing your regrets instead, maybe the most important and most meaningful moments in your real life would never have happened.

Like in my case, you might think all those years which slipped by went to waste. Actually, the reason why I kept forgetting about the linear storyline was because I was more focused on doing other things. I was busy living my life based on my own rules and spending quality time with people who matter to me because for me, life is never short if we live it well.

But for the purpose of this narrative, I didn't dwell on those other things since we all have different values. What's meaningful and important for some may not be meaningful and important for others. To each his own in defining what truly matters in one's life.

10. Being courageous is not just about being outwardly bold and brave. Courage could also be inward and silent. It could be in the form of:

- being truthful to yourself by acknowledging your unfiltered thoughts and feelings because these are your innermost desires and fears, not the answers you often tell people which they want to hear;

- taking full accountability for your life and not blaming others for your circumstances;

- charting your own life's trajectory even if it seems that you are the only one going in that direction;

- doing new, uncomfortable, painful or different things to achieve the target results even if the temptation to do easier things is more powerfully irresistible; and

- being unapologetically accepting and comfortable with yourself - no matter what.

Courageously single at 42 - I could not think of any other way I could have lived my life. But as to where I am going to steer the trajectory of my life in the coming years - and that includes whether I will have a Plus One or still a Plus None (among many other possibilities in life) - that is entirely up to me again.

*****

P.S. Curious to know if I have ever regretted not ending up with any of my past dates? When I bump into any of them, I always feel relieved that I didn't end up with any of them. Like with *boy* <*tab, tab, tab*> *friend*, the more I got to know myself better, the more I realized how different I am from each of my past dates. And if I have ever ended up with any of them, I could tell with 99.9999% accuracy we would have been separated after a few years. And I am sure they feel the same way too! I bet when they see me, they get some kind of validation they have picked the right woman to marry. See, I am even instrumental in making them realize that they have chosen their wives well!

P.P.S. Did I ever know how I want my eggs done? Yes! Sunny side up and well done. But if I am the one cooking the eggs, it's hard-boiled because it's the easiest to cook and it requires the least number of utensils to wash. ☺

AFTERWORD

Plus One Plus None is based on a true story and Zita hopes that through this sharing, you will realize what it is that you really want in your life and realize it within a shorter period than she did.

Zita's story is full of mishaps, challenges, mistakes, fears and imperfections, and it took her more than a decade to realize a lot of things, but it is what it is in real life. Sometimes it really takes several years (or even near the end of life for some) to gain real clarity, and it equally entails a lot of courage to admit all of these.

Zita could have simply said that she realized she was happy being single in her 30s and focused on the glamorous single life of travels, leisure activities and freedom. But no, she was brutally honest with her realizations along the way - that her efforts weren't good enough, that she didn't want to give up a lot of things and that she didn't want to risk her current state of contentment for something that is not guaranteed to be better. She has also never advocated single as being better than being married but instead, has repeatedly mentioned her high regard for parents and moms. In fact, she acknowledged that because of her fears, she may miss out on experiencing what she considers the greatest miracle of life (that of having a baby) and what she considers the most important achievement anyone can have in life (that of caring for and raising children well).

To nudge single women into action, I could have chosen a story of a single woman, who one day met her The One and got married, but that's what most movies and novels are made of already which may encourage single women to be lax about their single situation as they hope and wait in meeting their Plus One one fateful day. And so, I chose to tell Zita's story – a perfect story that could teach single women on what not to do if they want to get married within their timeline. I can't tell you anything else about Zita though as she prefers to remain anonymous consistent to her introvert nature.

Now that you have seen what could possibly happen in your life if you don't do regular self-checks, be brutally honest, process things faster, immediately act on your situation and follow through, may you be more conscious and be more purposeful with your actions and your time moving forward.

If you're still young, this may be difficult to grasp since it feels like you have all the time in the world, that things would happen according to plan and you're brimming with confidence that certain situations like ending up single at 40 won't ever happen to you but unexpected things could happen if you're not conscious about your actions and of time.

After finishing writing Zita's story, I talked to six other single women – five of them in their 40s and one in her 50s - and guess what? When they were all in their 20s, no one ever envisioned that they would end up single. They all expected to get married and have kids within their prime years. Upon further probing, four out of the six admitted that they didn't have any clear plans or timelines when they were in their prime years and they just coasted along their current lives. They only went out when they got asked out for dates and did not seek out friends to set them up when no one asked them out. The two others had a few serious relationships but none progressed to marriage for various personal reasons.

Two out of the six have gracefully embraced their single status, one is in a relationship whom she met through online dating (Yay!) and the remaining three are still hopeful to find a Plus One someday (although only one actively dates and the two others have decided to leave everything to fate).

With seven singles (including Zita), the sample size is too small to draw out any conclusions from but one thing is for sure - if you want to increase your chances of making things happen in your life, you have to actively do something about it. It's common sense but it's something we unfortunately sometimes forget, or we take for granted as we can easily blame other things for our circumstances.

At any age though, as Zita also shared in her narrative, you could still make anything happen if you really want to. Just recently, I attended a beautiful wedding of a 40-something couple. The guy wasn't the girl's type but she forced herself to still date him and she eventually realized how wonderful the guy is. The day after their wedding, the girl said she has never been happier in her life. *Awww*...

Zita's values, thoughts and circumstances may be very different from yours but the thought process of asking yourself a lot of whys in life, reflecting why you are behaving the way you are behaving, understanding where you are succeeding and failing, assessing what needs improvement, doing what needs to be done to achieve something within a timeline, and accepting the consequences of your decisions and actions - are all universal.

You can use all of these principles not just in your single situation but at whatever life stage you are in and even in your pursuit of your dreams and goals. It could be in the business idea you've been telling everyone you'll launch someday, the book you said you're going to write someday, the dream trip you said you're going to take one day, the MBA degree you said you're going to enroll in someday, or even for simple goals like starting an exercise habit or eating healthy which you often claim you would start doing but never get around really doing. Just remember - if you don't do the basic action to make these things happen, that someday would never come. Days could easily turn into weeks, weeks into months, months into years...

So, whatever it is you want to happen in your life, make sure you go beyond goal writing, planning, analyzing, claiming, wishing, praying, hoping, visualizing and waiting for things to happen in your life. Just make it happen.

P.S. Zita's story also teaches us not to easily judge a person who is unmarried. Just because a girl is unmarried, it does not mean that there are no guys pursuing her. Maybe she is simply not a date-and-tell person, or no one among her dates is passing her set standards, or she simply doesn't want to date.

It also reminds us not to give unsolicited advice to strangers or acquaintances such as why one should get married. Just because a single person is alone, it does not mean she is lonely. She might be happier, wiser and be in a better place than we are. In short, we should not be like the businessman in the fisherman story. We never know what if the joys of the ideal life we are chasing, are already being enjoyed by the person we are interrogating or advising. ☺

MESSAGE FROM THE AUTHOR

Thank you for reading Plus One Plus None.

Remember what Zita said about no amount of praying and wishing can make things happen if you don't do your part? That's what happened to me too as I was writing this book.

Writing a book has been in my goal list for the longest time and it was also in my prayer petitions. It was also my justification every time I got a new gadget saying I would be more inspired to write a book someday.

But guess what? After several years of upgrading gadgets, not even a single book idea was ever captured using any of them. That someday never came.

Yes, I had all the tech tools to write…

Yes, my goal was very clear in my head…

Yes, I visualized that someday it's going to happen…

And yes, I prayed a lot for it to happen …

But I actually never spent time doing the basic action to achieve my goal which is to write, nor have I spent time to even brainstorm on what to write. In short, everything was just wishful thinking.

Why did I never get around doing it? Because it was not easy - it was not easy to think of ideas, to organize thoughts, to write…

What was easier to do? All other things! It was easier to read, to surf the net, to sleep, to do gardening, to mop the floor, to de-clutter my closet, to find a missing box of paperclips, to patch a hole on my old shirt, to check food supplies in my cupboard if anything is about to expire… until there was no time left to write.

Days became weeks, weeks became months, months became years….

If I were dead serious about actually writing a book, I had to do something differently other than upgrading my gadgets, thinking about my goal, visualizing and praying.

So, I spent time writing - several hours every day - even if there were days when no idea came out of my head. I stayed up late at night and early hours in the morning to write even if I was dead tired at the end of a work day.

And just to finish this book project, for one whole year, I used my vacation leave credits so I could have more time to write Zita's story. Yes, I had to forego my usual travel adventures for one entire year.

Finally, after clocking in thousands of hours of writing, and several gadget upgrades, I finally completed this.

The moment I went beyond goal writing, praying, wishing and hoping, and really focused on doing, that's when my trajectory changed and took the right course.

So whatever it is you want in your life and it doesn't have to be love-related, you know what to do now. Just remember the life lessons from Zita and what's great is you don't have to go through the same long process and mistakes as she did. You can purposely start making things happen today. :-)

To send me a message, you may email me at **mao.emica@gmail.com**.

If you enjoyed this book, please **tell your friends** who might enjoy it too and **kindly leave a review on Amazon and/or Goodreads**. This is a self-published title and the only way for it to be discovered is through readers like you. Thank you.

Made in the USA
Middletown, DE
12 July 2021

44020288R00078